While most Americans are dreading getting older, and are literally scared of death, Dave Gallagher takes a counterintuitive view and reveals the essentials of happily embracing the second half of life. While there are definitely challenges after age fifty, this book reveals some important truths that add substance and perspective to growing older. If you want to finish life with purpose and hope, and not with a groan, as Psalm 90:9 expresses, join me in reading *Aging Successfully*!

—**Tom Shaw**
Vice President of Student Services
Moody Bible Institute of Chicago

Aging Successfully

Aging Successfully

How to Enjoy, Not Just Endure, the Second Half of Life

David P. Gallagher

WIPF & STOCK · Eugene, Oregon

AGING SUCCESSFULLY
How to Enjoy, Not Just Endure, the Second Half of Life

Wipf & Stock
An Imprint of Wipf and Stock Publishers
199 W. 8th Ave., Suite 3
Eugene, OR 97401

www.wipfandstock.com

ISBN 13: 978-1-61097-929-0

Manufactured in the U.S.A.

This book is dedicated to Ken Giacoletto, former President and CEO of Green Lake Conference Center in Green Lake, Wisconsin. Ken led this premier Christian conference and leadership training center through many storms for eighteen years and through his faithful example and godly integrity modeled servant leadership for Kingdom Impact around the world. When I concluded my last full time pastorate after forty years of ministry, Ken opened a new door of opportunity for me on staff at Green Lake Conference Center reminding me that aging successfully means we keep serving the Lord until we are in his glorious presence. Blessings upon you Ken and Peggy!

Contents

Acknowledgments

THIS BOOK would never have been written without the encouragement of so many people, who by their attitudes, responses, and actions reminded me of the importance of helping people to age successfully. I am particularly indebted to my wife Mary Ann, who patiently listened to me talk about the ideas for this book and helped with the book formatting. Together in marriage for forty-three years we both continue on life's journey of learning how to age successfully. Deepest gratitude goes to Dr. Gene A. Getz, Pastor Emeritus of Fellowship Bible Church North, Director of the Center for Church Renewal, Radio Host of Renewal Radio, and Adjunct Professor at Dallas Seminary. Dr. Getz was a professor of mine when I was a student at Moody Bible Institute many years ago. Gene helped shape my life for ministry. Forty-two years later I had the privilege of serving with Gene Getz on the Moody Alumni Board. He has unquestionably modeled how to age successfully. I extend great appreciation to Blythe Daniel, literary agent, marketing consultant, and owner of The Blythe Daniel Agency, Inc. Blythe kept encouraging me and persistently sought publishers for this manuscript. She always reminded me that there was a great need for a book such as this. I am very grateful to scores of colleagues and friends who helped with reading, proofing, and offering suggestions during the early stages of writing, including my mother-in-law Bertha Wetzig, Jean Cornelius, Bruce Finfrock, Paul Forsythe, and Chip Arn. I am also indebted to many lifelong friends in ministry who began in youth or Christian education ministry thirty or forty years ago and stayed the course, finding themselves now serving in Second Half Ministry local churches. None the least of these godly examples is Rod Toews at Peninsula Covenant Church in Redwood City, California; bless you Rod!

Introduction

L IFE'S JOURNEY is made up of mistakes and learning, waiting and growing, practicing patience and being persistent. There's an old Irish blessing that says, "You're not as young as you used to be, but you're not as old as you're going to be, so watch it!"

"Americans sixty-five and older are the fastest-growing segment of the population. 'In the past century, the number of American's over age sixty-five has increased twelvefold (from 3.1 to 37.9 million). By the year 2030, there will be 71.1 million people in America over age sixty-five.'[1] An American turns sixty every seven seconds."[2] Another factor causing the adult population over age fifty to increase is the extended life expectancies due to healthier lifestyles and advances in medical technology. This increasingly mature society is creating new trends and changing the way we think about older adults.

Aging Successfully offers suggestions for greater fulfillment and joy for people over fifty. It provides wisdom and time-tested counsel for a happy and highly productive second half of life.

1. U. S. Department of Health and Human Services, Administration on Aging, "A Profile on Older Americans, 2008," http://www.mowaa.org/ Document.Doc?id=69, p. 2, quoted in Hanson, *Baby Boomers and Beyond*, 4.

2. U. S. Census Bureau, "Selected Characteristics of Baby Boomers 42 to 60 Years Old in 2006," http://www.census.gov/population/www/socdemo/ age/2006%20Baby$Boomers.pdf, p. 20, quoted in Hanson, *Baby Boomers and Beyond*, 4. Computed by averaging 78 million baby boomers turning sixty for eighteen years.

Programs designed to reach people over the age of fifty are springing up everywhere. Universities, graduate schools, retail giants, developers—virtually every part of our society—see this age wave and are responding to it. The older adult population is exploding at three times the national population growth rate. I believe that those of us who are in their second half of life—those over age fifty—need a roadmap for enjoyable aging, especially as national programs for the aging grow more complex. Bureaucracy seems endless as older adults explore retirement, Social Security, health care, end-of-life issues, legal matters, issues relating to family and friends, and the list goes on. *Builders* (born between 1927 and 1945) and *Boomers* (born between 1946 and 1964) are two generations that need resources as they age and so do their children and grandchildren. We'll look at these age groups since men and women who fall into these generations—along with their caregivers and others assisting with the care of older adults—need the resources that are offered in this book.

But let's first look at what aging successfully is. Most people think of successful aging as staying young, healthy, engaged, fit, and having a positive attitude. They see successful aging as remaining independent, being wealthy, staying healthy, and being in control. But successful aging deals with many deeper issues. Aging successfully means that if you have aging parents who are growing weaker each day and you are pushed beyond human limits as a caregiver, God will give you the strength you need to face this challenge. Aging successfully also relies on the fact that even after forty years of work and finding that you must re-enter the job market, you can not only survive but also thrive in the process. And last, aging successfully implies that you can and will be able to help the terminally ill and care for those in need because you are learning to age productively and successfully.

Chances are that you've thought about or even discussed aging issues with your doctor or other professional. In this book you will find practical help with everything from finding relief from anxiety and burnout to making a new retirement budget. You will learn about self-care, home support, home delivered meal services, telephone reassurance, transportation services, independent living opportunities, assisted living, continuing care retirement, lifecare, adult day care, adult foster care, intermediate care, Alzheimer's care, hospice care, and respite care.

In the chapters that follow, I will share with you insights and principles that I gained in working with hundreds of people over the years. The principles come from personal experience, research, and helping people age successfully. I draw from my experience of ten years as senior pastor in an age-restricted community designed to reach people over age fifty. In this book, my goals are to:

- Remind you that the second half of life presents many opportunities, challenges, changes, and choices. Changes in finances, health, and family situations may cause us to lose a healthy perspective on aging.

- Alert you to the fact that procrastination is the thief of good intentions and that there is no substitute for solid preparation for our older years. Kids leaving for college or moving out of the house and retirement from work are major transitions that may cause unexpected stress unless there is careful thought and planning.

- Provide a biblical framework for aging. God places a high regard on aging.

- Encourage you to grow not only in chronological years but also as a whole person physically, emotionally, mentally, socially, and spiritually. Growing spiritually is a vital part of successful aging. Proverbs 16:31 tells us that God gives old age as a reward and that wisdom and understanding may come with aging.

- Offer a practical handbook explaining and simplifying vocabulary used by physicians, nurses, and social workers. People who are aging or have parents or friends who are aging need to know what resources are available. This practical handbook will help cut through the mountains of governmental bureaucracy and help people make wise, intelligent, and even godly decisions.

- Caution you to be aware of a preoccupation with materialism. Simple suggestions are offered on how to simplify your life and give to others out of your abundance. For example, we should be open to God's leading. We need to be aware of the needs of those around us. We need to be willing to help others. Spending reasonably helps fulfill the key words *perspective* and *balance.* Spending responsibly meets our personal needs now and saving methodically provides a plan for meeting future needs.

So why am I writing this book? I've been interested in the aging process ever since I was a child. Born in the city of Chicago, our family moved to Southern California when I was twelve years old. My parents were considered older parents when I was born—perhaps that is why I developed an interest in aging. As a young person, I had more than my share of friends my own age but I was always aware, intrigued, and even fascinated by the elderly.

When I was in junior high school, I developed a friendship with an older handicapped woman in our church. Miss Eberly drove an old station wagon, used a cane, and could hardly get around but I was drawn to her because she had a wonderful personality and a contagiously positive attitude about life. She seemed to have so much wisdom. She was a mentor and had learned so many lessons of life. She had integrity and seemed to know God in a special way. Though she had a serious handicap, she was joyful and very content inside. She had an inner peace and I wanted to learn about that.

In high school I had a friend named Ole Hugg who was the church janitor. After Sunday evening services he and I would go out to a small café and chat together. I learned about working hard and appreciating even the little things in life. He taught me about honesty and integrity. As he talked, he too seemed to overflow with wisdom. I was always in such a rush and he was always so calm. He could talk about the depression and hard times in a way that made me happy I was alive. He had learned some of the secrets of true happiness and I was interested in learning from him. I think deep down inside I knew that he had something few people had—true simplicity and inner joy. He could be happy simply by being with a kid like me and I think he truly enjoyed sharing his insights and lessons of life. We would talk about world problems, pollution, violence, war, religion, and politics and his age seemed to give everything a perspective and frame of reference that I didn't have.

Forty years have passed and I recently "transitioned" from full-time pastoral ministry (I don't like the word "retired"). I believe that I have learned a good bit about aging successfully, especially since the last ten years of my ministry were ministering to people over age fifty. I have grown to love elderly people and have a passion to help the aged not just endure, but also enjoy the later years of life. This passion comes from having seen the "untapped insight" in older adults sometimes being overlooked. It comes from seeing stereotypes and hearing too many jokes by people laughing at older adults and thinking they're "old school" and unable to understand or relate to the world today. This passion also comes from seeing elder abuse and watching people grow older without a plan for their elderly years.

We are all searching for meaning and hope, especially people over age fifty as they begin to evaluate their life. In the pages that follow, I will share some crucial concerns of successful aging, like keeping perspective and staying balanced between work and leisure, being active and being quiet, finding a good hobby, establishing solid friendships, being faithful in worship, and maintaining a healthy lifestyle. I will share ideas on enjoying midlife and preparing for the later years, maintaining a biblical view of aging, and understanding loss and grief. I'll also look at the importance of claiming God's promises and how to avoid the temptation of materialism. I'll offer a perspective on how to keep your spirits high and give specific ways to help relieve anxiety. As some people age they slowly lose hope. That's where faith comes in. A strong faith leads us to hope. Even those with a strong faith need encouragement that only God can give. There is a connection between having a strong faith and aging successfully.

Aging Successfully is designed to help you learn how to better prepare and live life to the fullest for the empty nest, grandchildren, retirement, changing energy levels and interests, serious illness, new use of time, marital changes (marriage may be different after twenty-five, thirty, forty, or fifty years with children gone), new roles, new opportunities, and

```
        5.              6.
    Maintain a      Understand           7.
   Biblical View   Loss and Grief       Claim
                                        God's
    4.                                 Promises
  Prepare for
  Later Years     Enjoying the          8.
                  Second Half of     Keep Your
    3.            Your Life          Spirits High
  Enjoy
  Midlife         Proverbs 16:31
                                        9.
                                      Relieve
    2.                                Anxiety
    Stay
  Balanced         1.           10.
                  Keep       Avoid the
               Perspective  Temptation of
                             Materialism
```

much more. This book offers practical suggestions for facing challenges in the second half of life, such as setting new priorities for life before or after retirement and caring for your spouse or parent in later years. Each chapter contains personal stories from my life and others who have walked in your shoes. But the book is more than pages of encouragement or advice. It will show you what to do in challenging situations and provide the answers you need to live a happy, more fulfilling second half of life.

As we age, we are faced with many choices about financial planning, retirement, long-term care insurance, health care, and many other issues. Some of those choices have enormous consequences. The point is that we need information, guidance, and insight to make wise choices and this book offers you that insight. So let's get started and learn some strategies to help on the journey of *Aging Successfully*!

1

Keep Perspective

And the peace of God, which transcends all understanding, will guard your hearts and your minds in Christ Jesus. Finally, brothers, whatever is true, whatever is noble, whatever is right, whatever is pure, whatever is lovely, whatever is admirable—if anything is excellent or praiseworthy—think about such things. Whatever you have learned or received or heard from me, or seen in me—put it into practice. And the God of peace will be with you. I rejoice greatly in the Lord that at last you have renewed your concern for me. Indeed, you have been concerned, but you had no opportunity to show it. I am not saying this because I am in need, for I have learned to be content whatever the circumstances. (Phil 4:7–11)

PERSPECTIVE HELPS US SEE THE BIGGER PICTURE WHEN WE FACE CHALLENGES

THE SECOND half of life is sometimes like a roller coaster ride. After age fifty, life may seem to be a series of mountaintop experiences sometimes followed by valleys of great challenges.

I was approaching my fortieth birthday. Thirty was a struggle for me but forty—no way. I wanted little done or said about my fortieth birthday. We had a small family dinner and some gifts were given. For me it was, "Let's get through this as quietly and quickly as possible." A very dear friend gave me a little gift. I did not realize it at the time, but that little gift was very significant. In fact, it took me about ten years to realize its significance. It was a coffee mug with the words, "Life Begins at 40" printed on it. You've seen them. Frankly, it was only out of politeness that I said thank you to her, for I really didn't like the thought of being forty, and I certainly was not going to use that little cup that would remind me every day that I was "over forty." So I quietly and unassumingly put the little cup on the top shelf of our kitchen cabinet (clear in the back). The little cup remained there for a long time, actually for many years. Without realizing it, a decade had passed. I was approaching fifty, but honestly, I still felt like I was twenty. After my birthday celebration was over and everyone left or went to bed, I remembered that little cup. I quietly strolled over to the kitchen and reached way back behind the other cups and found the "Life Begins at 40" cup. I looked at it through new eyes. I had learned a very important lesson about life itself.

To a ten-year-old, someone sixteen is "old." To a sixty-year-old person, someone fifty is "young." Age is not a numerical value but a mindset, an attitude, a lifestyle, an outlook. In life there are ups and downs. We learn to take it one day at a time. We learn to take the good with the bad. We learn that life really is fragile. Yes, life is unfair at times, but how we respond is the key. How we respond is sort of the great equalizer to help us keep perspective and a positive attitude—no matter what.

In the game of golf, some golfers have a "handicap." The handicap equalizes golfers so the average golfer has opportunity to golf with the excellent golfer. This equalizing puts players on the same playing field so to speak. It allows the poor or average golfer an opportunity to set goals from his or her own previous scores. Without that equalizer, the poor or average golfer's viewpoint, attitude, or perspective could be, "What's the use of golfing—I have no possible chance of getting a good score." The golfer would have no motivation. That defeatist perspective would take all of the joy out of golfing. Perspective helps create our attitude.

An eighty-two-year-old male golfer was preparing to hit the ball from the red ladies' tee on the first hole, right in front of the pro shop. As he began his backstroke, a voice boomed over the public address system: "Would the man hitting his ball from the ladies' tee, please move it back to the men's tee?!" He glared over his shoulder then began again to prepare to hit the ball. The loudspeaker again shattered the silence, repeating, "Will the man hitting the ball from the ladies' tee, please move it back to the white, men's tee?!" At that, the man turned and faced the clubhouse. Cupping his hands around his mouth he hollered, "Will the man in the clubhouse please be quiet, so I can take my SECOND shot?!"

A number of years ago I had a serious ear infection. I went to a specialist who prescribed medication and, after time, the infection cleared up. Following that process, I had my hearing checked just as a precaution. My hearing seemed perfect to me. I certainly didn't feel like I had any hearing loss but since I had recently recovered from a serious infection, my physician wanted to double check. The audiologist completed the procedure and told me that I had some hearing loss. I was sure that my hearing was just fine and questioned the test results. I was given another exam and the results showed that I had no hearing loss. My hearing was the same after each exam but my feelings were very different after each procedure. My attitude and perspective were changed by the circumstances. My hearing had not changed, but my response changed because I thought the circumstances had changed. And if I had hearing loss that would mean that I would be faced with an opportunity to decide to become a bitter person or to grow and become a better person.

Isn't it interesting how our perspective changes as we age? For example, for years I noticed the slanted metal bars in handicapped showers and restrooms, and thought they were for someone else. I'd see those metal brackets on the walls and was glad that I did not need to use them. Then one day when we were in a motel and I was taking a shower I turned around abruptly and found myself instinctively grabbing one of the brackets! It was at that moment that I realized that I was not twenty-five anymore; in fact, I was in the second half of my life and had better begin accepting that reality.

Our thinking greatly influences our perspective. Bad feelings are the result of distorted, negative thinking. Our thoughts determine our feelings, our feelings set our moods, and our moods lead us to our actions. You feel the way you do right now because of thoughts you are thinking right now. I love to be with happy, positive people. I do not enjoy being around cranky, negative people. Why? Because the moods of others directly affect my moods. Philippians 4:8 says, "Finally, brothers, whatever is true, whatever is noble, whatever is right, whatever is pure, whatever is lovely, whatever is admirable—if anything is excellent or praiseworthy—think about such things."

Once when I was with a patient before surgery, I intended to read some scripture and offer a word of encouragement and prayer for God's guidance and peace. After I read and said a few words of encouragement, I was just about to pray when a nurse came to the man's bed. She checked his chart, made sure that everything was in order, and told me that he would be going to surgery very shortly. The doctor and the nurse had said earlier that attitude was extremely important prior to surgery. I remember the man saying over and over to me and to his wife that he was sure that he would not come out of surgery alive. I also remember that nurse who came in. She leaned over the bed and looked right into his eyes and she said very sternly, "No more of that negative talk now. I've been a nurse for over fifteen years and know that the attitude going into surgery greatly impacts the results and recovery." Attitude! Perspective! Today, whatever the situation—grasp the positive attitude. Whatever your situation, why not say, "I will choose to have a positive attitude?" He came through surgery just fine.

When I woke up this morning the sun was up and shining. I couldn't help but think of how good God is every day. I didn't worry about the sun coming up; I knew it would come up—it always does. Why? Because God is faithful. The rising sun reminded me of God's faithfulness. God's faithfulness is a continued theme in scripture. God's faithfulness means that I have assurance of salvation and forgiveness (John 10:27–30; 1 John 1:9) and it assures me that he will provide me strength as I face loss, sorrow, loneliness, and affliction (1 Pet 4:12–13). It is important to remember that God's faithfulness means that I can have peace and victory (1 Cor 10:13) and that I have spiritual blessings from a sovereign God (1 Cor 1:9; Ps 84:11–12). God's faithfulness also means that I can reflect God's love and grace in my life as I yield my life to him (Gal 5:22–23). All of this helps form my perspective.

LOSS OF PERSPECTIVE MAY LEAD
TO DEPRESSION

Sometimes if we lose perspective and do not stay balanced in our life, depression may creep in. We have a tendency of overdoing good things. We eat too much or push ourselves too hard. The Bible speaks about moderation in all things to help us stay balanced (Phil 4:5–6 KJV). Depression is a loss of pleasure and enjoyment in life. It's a feeling of sadness, disappointment, and being very alone. Depression may manifest itself by physical discomfort, aches, pains, fatigue, poor digestion, and sleep disorders. Webster's defines it as "that which causes you to sink or be low in spirit; to be sad, dejected, lowering of activity and vitality, and mood swings. Depression is a withdrawal from people activities."[1]

Depression is one of the most common mental health challenges. But you might feel that depression is just a normal part of aging, so you don't seek treatment for this illness. Depression can be caused by poor eating habits, not getting enough rest, reaction to drugs (toxic depression), physical depression related to glands, infections of the brain and nervous system, hypoglycemia, repression of anger and anger turned inward, self-pity and self-blame or poor self-image, or faulty behavior and faulty thinking.[2] Simply being aware of a situation that can put you or your spouse at risk for depression can help you make sure you seek treatment if needed. These situations include:

- Retirement or other changes in role or status
- Financial issues
- Loss through death or relocation of family, friends, or pets

1. Webster's New Collegiate Dictionary, 1980 ed., s.v. "depression."
2. Burke, "Preventing Depression," 64.

- Loss or perceived loss of function or capabilities
- Chronic illness or pain[3]

Also, take note if you or your spouse shows any of these signs of depression:

- Constant or pervasive sadness
- Difficulty concentrating or making decisions
- Loss of interest in hobbies, friends, or activities
- Change in sleeping habits
- Sudden weight loss or gain
- Frequent visits to the doctor
- Statements such as "You'd be better off without me" or "I don't want to be a burden"[4]

My wife and I were serving in a church in Santa Monica, California. It was a wonderful time in our lives. We lived eleven blocks from the beach and the church was only ten blocks from the beach. We'd been there for quite a number of years and were loved and well taken care of by the church family. But all of a sudden, for apparently no reason, my wife became a bit depressed. She tried to shake it but it would not go away. In fact, her darkness grew deeper and deeper each day. She went to our family physician who was a member of our church and he could find no physical reason for her change. After another visit to our family physician, she went to a gynecologist, and the gynecologist found no reason for the depression. It was back to our family physician and then the two of us went to a fine Christian psychologist at a well-known psychological center, which to our dismay turned up absolutely nothing. She went to a specialist who

3. Ibid.
4. Ibid.

also confirmed that she could find absolutely nothing that might cause this change.

My wife's entire personality was changing day by day and she seemed to be falling deeper and deeper into a huge dark hole. I hardly knew her anymore. She took a leave of absence from her job. I began cutting back my hours to spend more time with her. I will never forget one afternoon when I walked in the front door of our apartment and did not hear her voice greeting me. I walked down the long hallway into our master bedroom and saw her sitting in a chair staring at nothing. The drapes were closed, the television was not on; not even a light was on. She was just sitting there and didn't even acknowledge my presence. I kneeled down in front of her and softly spoke words of encouragement and comfort. I reminded her that we would get through this together—that we would keep trying until we found the answer to this crippling depression. Weeks went by and we saw no progress. More visits to doctors only to hear that there was no reason for this behavior. She of course stopped attending worship and even stopped going outside—she wanted to see no one. Since we lived only two blocks from the church I suggested that she come late to worship and try just slipping up into the balcony and see how it felt. From the platform I saw her slip in but only for a few moments—then she got up and left. Her feelings were simply overwhelming and it was changing our lives.

The breakthrough came when she decided to return to our family doctor. As she was leaving the doctor's office, his nurse prodded my wife to go back to the gynecologist and insist that she be given estrogen. Hesitantly she made the appointment and insisted that she be given estrogen. The doctor was quick to respond to her that she had already done tests for that and found it was not needed. However, the doctor was willing to give it a try. Within a few days on estrogen, her personality was changing for the good and within two weeks she was back to her old self.

During my research I discovered that some depression involves what's going on inside, and some involves what's going on outside. Chemical imbalance in the brain can cause depression. Life events can trigger depression. In addition, the death of a loved one, a strained relationship, drugs, a transition, or even the birth of a baby or grandchild can cause depression and deep grief. When we experience depression, we need help—help from God, his Word, and our friends. Sometimes we need help from a pastor, counselor, or physician.

You can take some specific positive practical steps to climb out of depression—especially if you're simply not experiencing the joy you once knew. If that statement describes how you or your spouse feels, try these ideas:

- Give praise. Rejoicing in the Lord is closely linked in scripture with praising the Lord: "May all who are godly rejoice in the Lord and praise His holy name!" (Ps 97:12 NLT). It's easy to become nearsighted and see only your "problems." Getting outside, even if only for a simple walk around the block can be a very healthy experience. Being with friends at church, singing praise to the Lord, and engaging in good fellowship can do wonders.

- Read positive scriptures. Jeremiah is often called the weeping prophet. He wrote: "When I discovered your words, I devoured them. They are my joy and my heart's delight" (Jer 15:16 NLT). Many of the Psalms also lift the discouraged and depressed heart.

- Pray. Okay, so this sounds cliché. Yet prayer is an

amazing means of fighting depression and increasing joy in your life. Jesus said, "You haven't done this before. Ask, using my name, and you will receive, and you will have abundant joy" (John 16:24 NLT).

- Obey and serve God. Again, Jesus pointed out the benefits: "When you obey my commandments, you remain in my love, just as I obey my Father's commandments and remain in his love. I have told you these things so that you will be filled with my joy. Yes, your joy will overflow!" (John 15:10–11 NLT).

Additionally, take some practical actions, such as exercising, abdominal breathing, mental relaxation, meditation, muscle relaxation, a warm bath, listening to music, doing something for others, talking it out, family support, revising a daily schedule, or just being with good friends for some fun.[5]

At some time, everyone experiences a little depression. We feel down on life and down on ourselves. Sometimes after a bad day or a bad golf game, our moods change briefly. Sometimes depression lingers on. We sometimes just can't seem to get back up and shake it off.

Keep a positive perspective on your roller coaster ride. If you are depressed or experiencing grief, you need people who really care. In the Old Testament, the Bible tells us that the psalmist David experienced depression and fear. Find insight from Psalms 42 and 43, where the psalmist writes about the seeming cycle of depression. The cycle begins with thoughts and moves on to feelings. As mentioned earlier there are thoughts that cause feelings, which create a mood, and the mood creates the attitude and action. When we think silly, happy thoughts, we begin to smile. If we think of

5. "Stress Without Distress," 48.

a sad event and begin to think negatively, we begin to feel depressed. Negative thoughts cause emotional turmoil. Nearly all of the time, such thoughts are distortions.

David applied some basic and simple principles to his life in dealing with depression. Psalm 42 helps us with some of these principles. David remembered how God had helped in the past: "These things I remember as I pour out my soul. . . . therefore I will remember" (Ps 42:4, 6). If you are depressed, lonely, or experiencing grief, remember a time when you were happy. I have wonderful memories from every congregation in which I have served. I keep the wonderful memories before me through pictures in albums and those hanging on a wall in my study. I save the precious notes, letters, and cards that have been given to me over the years. David remembered how God had helped him in the past. We must remember how God has cared for us in the past.

David practiced hope and praise, even during times of discouragement: "Why are you downcast, O my soul? Why so disturbed within me? Put your hope in God, for I will yet praise Him, my Savior and my God" (Pss 42:5–6a, 11; 43:5 KJV). If you are experiencing depression, discouragement, and grief try using a hymnal to read or sing some of the wonderful old hymns and gospel songs of the church. If you are down, lonely, or discouraged, offer praise and remember the good things God has done. David remembered what God had done and offered hopeful praise.

David knew that God was his stronghold, his strength, and the light at the end of the *tunnel*. David said of God, "You are God my stronghold" (Ps 43:2a KJV). Sometimes to gain victory over depression, we must remember what God has done and is now doing. We will need to practice hope and praise. We will need to claim the victory of God who is our strength and victory.

David knew there was light and truth to guide him, even though he might not see it at that moment: "Send forth your light and your truth, let them guide me; let them bring me to your holy mountain, to the place where you dwell" (Ps 43:3 KJV). God's Word has power to help us each day. The Holy Spirit indwells with power. We may not see the end right now, but we must do as David did. David remembered what God had done. David practiced hope and praise. David claimed that God is strength.

David went to the altar of God to find joy and delight: "These things I remember as I pour out my soul: how I used to go with the multitude, leading the procession to the house of God, with shouts of joy and thanksgiving among the festive throng. Why are you downcast, O my soul? Why so disturbed within me? Put your hope in God, for I will yet praise him, my Savior and my God" (Ps 42:4–6a KJV). God desires that we place our lives on the altar.

Today you have a choice, to begin your journey into aging with a positive healthy mindset and to gain hope from the Bible and from the wisdom of those who have already taken this journey. At the very start, thank God for this book knowing that it is intended to be a daily resource for strength, hope, and encouragement.

Reflections about God, Faith, and Trials

To make this more personal, here are some questions to think about:

1. How has God shown his faithfulness to you, to your family, at your job, or with material provisions?

2. What aspects of faith did a recent trial bring about in your faith?

3. What wisdom did you gain through this trial?

4. What is the relationship between crisis and faith in your life?

2

Stay Balanced

It is good to grasp the one and not let go of the other.
The man who fears God will avoid all [extremes].
(Eccl 7:18, brackets in original)

Let your gentleness [self-control] be evident to all. The
Lord is near. (Phil 4:5, brackets mine)

BALANCING LIFE'S PRIORITIES

A NOTHER VERY important part of aging successfully is
balancing priorities. As people age we see that some become more quiet, soft, sweet, and flexible, and we see others
that become more harsh, brittle, and cranky. Priorities and
pressures of life impact people in different ways and people
respond in different ways. I read a little quip about a certain
village where somebody took the liberty of adding to the sign
on the outskirts of the town: "Population 500—1 grouch."

Some older people have a great vision for the future,
while others refuse to live in the present and insist on living in
the past. Some enjoy active, healthy lives, while others seemingly suffer pain and grief constantly. Some have material
wealth, while others seem to be destined (or determined) to

a life of poverty and loneliness. Some are growing spiritually, and others are stagnant and spiritually dry. I have noticed in older adults that what people are today will only intensify as they age. However, they do have a choice. A key to aging successfully is to know how to balance life's priorities even when facing great challenges. I didn't say that would be easy, but it is achievable.

Balance is steadiness, faithfulness, or stability. Balance involves staying the course and not being swayed by others. One would think that having lived forty-five or fifty years we would have learned the importance of balance, but often that is not the case. As we age, it becomes important that we develop qualities of stability, steadiness, faithfulness, and consistency, and that we learn to focus on what is important in life. The opposite of these qualities is instability or impulsiveness. The aging process brings with it the opportunity to learn lessons in life, not repeating the same mistakes.

For example, many young people overextend themselves, purchasing a myriad of things only to discard a few months later. As we age, we realize that we do not need many things and, at some point, we begin putting them in the garage. A child would eat chocolate cake and ice cream for breakfast, lunch, and dinner. A high school or college student would eat pizza and ice cream at midnight. However, as we mature we learn the importance of a balanced diet and balance in life.

I heard a little story that after starting a new diet, a man altered his drive to the golf course to avoid passing his favorite bakery. But, one morning, he accidently drove by the bakery and as he approached, there in the window were a host of goodies. He felt this was no accident, so he prayed, "Lord, it's up to you, if you want me to have any of those delicious goodies, please create a parking place for me directly in front of the bakery." And sure enough, on the eighth time around the block, there it was!

We may get into trouble when we mature chronologically, but not mentally, emotionally, financially, or spiritually. Take some time to evaluate what you are reading, watching on television, what you are eating and drinking, and where you spend your time. Glance through your checkbook and note where and how you spend your money. Aging successfully involves maintaining balance in life.

We've all heard the stories of those going through a midlife crisis. As we pass midlife and grow into our older adult years, we face challenges. As we face these challenges, we may act impulsively, and of course there are consequences to acting on impulse. Sometimes we say foolish things that later we regret.

Sometimes in a panic, we even may lose touch with reality. The joke is told of a man who faced such challenges.

An older man was driving down the freeway when his cell phone rang. Answering, he heard his wife's voice urgently warning him, "Herman, I just heard on the news that there's some crazy man driving a car the wrong way on Highway 280. Please be careful!" "Hazel!" said Herman, "It's not just one car! There are hundreds of them!" We chuckle at that story and yet it makes a point that sometimes we do not face up to reality. Admittedly, that joke is ridiculous but if we are honest, we must admit that we sometimes do some rather odd things. I guess we all have our neuroses and most of us act as though we will live forever. We eat, drive, and live as though life has no end.

The fact is that our earthly days are limited and it is important that we use our time wisely. We need to spend our money wisely. We need to eat and exercise wisely. We need to cultivate our friendships wisely. In a word: We need to live a balanced life.

THE BOOMER GENERATION

The changing age demographics will not only affect our society, but will cause us to rethink our goals, purposes, and challenges of life in its various stages.[1]

My wife and I live in an age-restricted community designed to attract Boomers. I served as the lead pastor in another age-restricted community that is specifically designed to attract Builders. Each community is very different and the amenities and strategies to draw residents are unique to attract either Boomers or Builders. Just as there are unique age characteristics for children and youth, so there are unique interests and characteristics for Boomers and Builders.

Boomers are adults born between 1946 and 1964. They were impacted by what went on in the 1950s, 1960s, and 1970s. Most Boomers well remember the birth of rock 'n' roll and find themselves slipping into nostalgia when they hear a Chuck Berry, Little Richard, Elvis, or Beatles song. Boomers experienced the phenomena of yuppies and Vietnam. Boomers remember the Cold War and experienced economic affluence. Boomers lived during the birth of the Civil Rights Movement. They remember Watergate and the Nixon resignation.[2]

Unlike the Builders, many Boomers are missing the spiritual dynamic. Boomers are generally very active physically. For example, I was asked to go golfing with a friend who recently retired and moved to our area. I was just over fifty at the time. We set the time at 2:00 p.m. When we met

1. Dychtwald and Flower, *Age Wave*, 8.
2. McIntosh, *One Church Four Generations*, 71–91.

and exchanged greetings, I asked what he had been doing throughout the day. He told me that he had played tennis in the morning, followed by a light lunch with his wife. He was on a softball team and had played right up until 2:00 p.m., at which time he was now ready to play a round of golf with me. I was amazed! This vividly reinforced the fact that we certainly may age triumphantly! Believe it or not, after our golf game, he asked me if he would see me at the fitness center that evening.

Most Boomers are still working, some are retired, but nearly all have a wide variety of interests and a great deal of energy and creativity. Here are just a few of the activities and interests of Boomers: computers, rock climbing, inline skating, art, book review clubs, ceramics, gardening, stitching, photo and video clubs, radio control airplane flyers, stained glass, woodcrafters, motorcycling, RVing, singles clubs, social groups, travel clubs, bicycling, billiards, bocce ball, bowling, dance, golf, horseshoes, hiking, walking, kayaking, lawn bowling, mountain biking, roller blading, sailing, scuba diving, softball, swimming, tennis, table tennis, water polo, drama/comedy clubs, music, dominoes, Scrabble, bridge, canasta, cribbage, and pinochle. This list could be much longer, but I've just taken these activities and clubs right out of the Sun City Grand Boomer community's monthly newspaper, *Grand Times*, in Surprise, Arizona.

A close friend of ours worked as Chief Financial Officer at a Christian publishing company for over forty years. When he retired, he and his wife moved to Arizona and began attending our church. It wasn't long before we became good friends and I learned of one of his hobbies. He loved to create DVDs of memorable occasions. After forty years of working with numbers this gave him the opportunity to really do what he loved to do—show creativity in making DVDs.

At Christmastime our church gathered care items to put in Christmas stockings to send to soldiers in Iraq. My friend prepared an amazing DVD showing the folks who filled over three hundred Christmas stockings, packed them into boxes, and shipped them overseas.

Many of our friends love golfing, many love being on the softball team. Others like being on the drama team at our church and some enjoy being in the community Broadway show performed each year. The point is that Boomers are extremely active people.

In the book *Generation Ageless*, J. Walker Smith and Ann Clurman point out that there are a number of commonalities among Boomers as a general group. For example, if you were born between 1946 and 1964, chances are that you think in terms of things related to immortality and morality. Boomers seem to be caught up with self-perceptions about youthfulness, impact, possibility, and passion as well as zealous self-interests related to health, vitality, and social connections, especially with grandchildren.[3]

Words like impact, possibility, passion, zealous, health, vitality, and grandchildren are all Boomer concepts. Understanding this helps us understand the aging process. For the Boomer the word is not "retirement," rather the word is "transition." Boomers do not retire from life; they transition from work. With people living so much longer today than in years past many Boomers return to some other form of part-time or full-time work. One well-known home building company has the motto, "Retire from work—not life." That's exactly what is in the mind of the Boomer.

3. Smith and Clurman, *Generation Ageless*, 116.

Bionic aids and sports medicine products, and home health care and integrated medicine specialists have literally changed the twenty-first century second half of life.[4]

Aging successfully involves paying attention to all aspects of life: our physical, mental, social, emotional, and spiritual life. There are hundreds if not thousands of ways to begin to age successfully and that is what this book is all about.

Trends that May Be Coming for Boomers

"Americans sixty-five and older are the fastest-growing segment of the population. 'In the past century, the number of American's over age sixty-five has increased twelvefold (from 3.1 to 37.9 million). By the year 2030, there will be 71.1 million people in America over age sixty-five.'[5] An American turns sixty every seven seconds."[6]

"The United States Social Security Administration expects to receive ten thousand applications per day for the next twenty years just for members of the baby boomer generation who are reaching ages of entitlement."[7]

None of us can predict what adult church ministry will be like five or ten years from now, but demographic and social trends do reveal some realistic possibilities. As we read

4. An excellent resource on future trends for this, the second half of life, is Brent Green's *Marketing to Leading-Edge Baby Boomers*, 67–69.

5. U. S. Department of Health and Human Services, Administration on Aging, "A Profile on Older Americans, 2008," http://www.mowaa.org/Document.Doc?id=69, p. 2, quoted in Hanson, *Baby Boomers and Beyond*, 4.

6. U. S. Census Bureau, "Selected Characteristics of Baby Boomers 42 to 60 Years Old in 2006," http://www.census.gov/population/www/socdemo/age/2006%20Baby$Boomers.pdf, p. 20, quoted in Hanson, *Baby Boomers and Beyond*, 4. Computed by averaging 78 million baby boomers turning sixty for eighteen years.

7. Houston and Parker, *Vision for the Aging Church*, 35.

books like *Marketing to Leading-Edge Baby Boomers* by Brent Green and glean articles found on web sites like Christian Association Serving Adults (www.gocasa.org) we begin to get a sense of direction. Gleaning from these two sources, twelve realistic possibilities start to unfold in the future:

1. Breakdown of traditional paradigms: One-third or more of all Boomers will be unable to pay the costs of health care and there will be an overstressed Medicare system. Churches and other social organizations across the nation will have unprecedented opportunities to help people in need, particularly the elderly.

2. Increased generational conflict: We will see expanding social alienation between the older and the younger in our society and in our churches. Society will become dangerously polarized and churches will need to give serious attention to teaching biblical principles about aging.

3. Specialized psychological services, financial planning, and Elder Law specialists: Pastors and counselors will have the opportunity to promote optimistic mental health for middle age and older adults. More specialized counseling agencies will be available for an aging population and small group ministries in churches will need to focus on meeting needs. Elder Law is a relatively new area of legal practice that focuses on the legal needs of older adults and incapacitated people and their families. As people grow older they need to look seriously at not only the financial and health issues ahead, but also take steps to ensure that things are in order legally.

4. Greater emphasis on good nutrition: Restaurants will need to respond to the massive demographic changes. Menus will move from offering one or two "senior op-

tions" to a much larger variety of options for nutrition-ally conscious adults.

5. More and better physical fitness: Fitness centers will of-fer more programs for middle age and older adults who will want and need joint-friendly aerobic equipment and relaxation programs.

6. Many more bionic aids: Nearly invisible hearing aids and other technology will help control and hide the ap-pearance of disabilities.

7. More trendy upscale retirement communities: Many middle age adults (Boomers) will relocate to com-munities designed to accommodate active adults, and older adults (Builders) will look for communities de-signed to accommodate wheelchairs and other physi-cally disabling conditions. The concept of "lifecare" communities will expand. Lifecare is a comprehensive, pay-one-price concept for providing long-term care for a controlled cost. Residents pay a one-time entrance fee and a monthly service fee based on the square footage of the living unit they select. There will be more home health care and group homes for the aging.

8. Travel will focus more on adventure and education: Christian travel groups like Educational Opportunities (EO) in Lakeland, Florida (http://www.eo.travelwithus. com/) already offer tours with a specific purpose.

9. Generation-specific publications: These publications will keep adults informed about the newest innovations designed to make life easier and more pleasant and will also give details about medical breakthroughs.

10. Advancements in marketing strategies to direct and build relationships: Technology will allow direct marketing to become extremely personal. The church will surely need to tap into new technology for personalized follow-up of their members and friends.

11. Survival strategies for men and women who are widowed, divorced, or without partners: Clergy and church leadership teams may have amazing opportunities for ministry to singles, widowed, and divorced among the aging population.

12. An increased unwillingness to surrender to the aging process: Technology will continue to allow people to live longer and opt to replace nearly any and every limb or organ needed. Aging adults will continue to strive for a healthier, more active lifestyle.[8]

Rather than thinking of the aging process as a slowdown time, realize that aging and retirement or transition from full-time work brings with it the opportunity to devote your time to learning, serving, planning, and living a more active and exciting life. Even in economically challenging times, you may explore new types of work. This could be the time to pursue new training for new and exciting opportunities.

THE BUILDERS GENERATION

Builders were born between 1927 and 1945. Generally speaking their lifestyle is somewhat slower than the Boomers but there are many striking exceptions. Some eighty-year-olds are far more physically active and mentally alert than some fifty-year-olds!

8. Green, *Marketing to Leading-Edge Baby Boomers*, 151–55.

Churches and other service and social organizations come up with all kinds of labels and standards by which they define adults in their second half of life. Some use phrases like "older adults," "elderly," "senior citizens," "silver circle," or "golden-agers." I've served in churches where more interesting names were used, such as "speeders—over 55," "pacemakers," and "friendship group." Many churches today use the term "second half ministry." One thing seems clear, Boomers do not like words like "older," "elderly," or "senior adult" and Builders are much more open to such terms. Whatever the nomenclature, it does not represent a numerical age or category. Twenty-first century middle age or older adult has more to do with attitude and lifestyle. Older adults do not think of themselves as old, older, or declining. They view themselves as alive, vibrant, active, and moving forward to accomplish things they've always wanted to do but never had the time.

A Proud Senior Citizen

I'm a senior citizen and proud of it—I'm the life of the party, even when it lasts until 8:00 p.m. I'm very good at opening childproof caps with a hammer. I'm usually interested in going home before I get to where I am going. I'm the first one to find the bathroom wherever I go. I'm awake many hours before my body allows me to get up. I'm smiling all the time because I cannot hear a word you're saying. I'm very good at telling stories, over and over and over and over again. I'm aware that other people's grandchildren are not as bright as mine. I'm not grouchy; I just don't like traffic, waiting, crowds, children, politicians . . . I'm wrinkled, saggy, lumpy, and that's just my left leg. I'm realizing that aging is not for sissies. If you are what you eat, I'm Shredded Wheat and

All-Bran®. I'm wondering, if you're only as old as you feel, how could I be alive at one hundred fifty? I'm supporting all movements now, by eating bran, prunes, and raisins. I'm a senior citizen, and I think I am having the time of my life.

Builders may be the most neglected group in churches today because most churches place such a strong focus on reaching younger people. That could prove to be a serious mistake for many reasons, none the least being that Builders have amazing wisdom to bring to the church. Builders need to share their wisdom and younger groups need to grasp their wisdom. They are the group who went through the 1920s, 1930s, and 1940s. This group remembers World War I, the Roaring Twenties, and the Great Depression. During the ten years I served as lead pastor in the two-generation church made up of Boomers and Builders, I placed a strong focus on home visitation. In fact, during those ten years my wife and I made over five thousand visits. At each visit we heard amazing stories about the Great Depression, Pearl Harbor and World War II, rationing, the Korean War, and more. I could write a book on the stories I heard from those home and hospital visits. Builders are hard workers and have amazing loyalty. They are frugal and at the same time are amazing givers. Builders generally were raised in a religious era. These folks are committed to the church and missionary endeavors around the world.

Builders enjoy many of the activities Boomers enjoy, such as computers, art, book review clubs, ceramics, gardening, stitching, photo and video clubs, stained glass, woodcrafters, RVing, singles clubs, travel, billiards, bocce ball, bowling, dance, golf, horseshoes, walking, lawn bowling, swimming, table tennis, drama/comedy clubs, music, dominoes, Scrabble, bridge, canasta, cribbage, and pinochle.

Because of physical limitations, they are not as free to participate in some of the more strenuous activities. Of course, there are exceptions. An eighty-year-old woman who attends our church loves hiking. She is in the Builder generation and she has boundless energy. In fact, she loves hiking and hikes the Grand Canyon every year. She could easily out hike most Boomers and probably out hike most Gen Xers (born 1965 to 1983) and perhaps most Millennials (born 1984 to 2002).

However, many Builders are beginning to face health challenges. It is not uncommon for Builders to have frequent visits to the doctor, take numerous daily prescriptions, and have surgeries for knee replacement, hip replacement, cataract and lens implants, and various other surgical procedures. Builders may be faced with disorders of the eyes, ears, heart, blood, respiratory system, digestive system, urinary track, and many other health challenges. Aging Builders may become unsteady and have a greater propensity to fall when moving around at home or out in public. Some may fall numerous times, but because of their extreme spirit of personal independence, refuse to use a cane or walker even when needed.

The person who is aging successfully understands the various seasons of life and tries to prepare for the physical, mental, emotional, social, and spiritual changes that come. For example, I offer a checklist in chapter five that helps you determine if you are independent, need help to perform a task, or are unable to do so at all. Depending on your needs and limitations, you may need assisted living, home care, rehabilitation, or skilled nursing care. It may be that all you need right now is a simple medical alert that you wear around your neck in case you do fall. Or perhaps a walker or cane is needed to give you a little steadiness.

I remember a single older man in our church family who lost his wife and was living alone. He began falling at his house but resisted my suggestion to use a cane to steady himself or to wear a simple devise with an alert button to call for help if he ever fell. He thought he wasn't ready for either, but was limiting his mobility and safety, thereby hindering his own peace of mind and well-being. Once he accepted the idea of both of these helpful aides he began to show the joy he once knew. He was back in worship and getting around quite well.

Someone wrote this little quip titled "Life Begins at 80." The first eighty years are the hardest. The second eighty are a succession of birthday parties. Once you reach eighty, everyone wants to carry your luggage and help you up the steps. If you forget your name or anybody else's name, or your own telephone number, or promise to be three places at the same time, or you can't remember how many grandchildren you have, you need only explain that you are eighty. Being eighty is a lot better than being seventy. At seventy people are mad at you for everything. At eighty, you have a perfect excuse no matter what you do. If you act foolishly, it's just your second childhood. Everybody is looking for symptoms of softening of the brain. Being seventy is no fun at all. At that age, they expect you to retire to a house in Florida and complain about your arthritis (they use to call it lumbago) and you ask everybody to stop mumbling because you can't understand them. (Actually, your hearing is about 50 percent gone). If you survive until you are eighty, everyone is surprised that you're still alive and they treat you with respect just for having lived so long. Actually, they seem surprised that you can even walk and talk sensibly. So please, friends, just try to make it to eighty. It's the best time of life. People will forgive you for anything. If you ask me—life begins at eighty!

Practical Steps to Take Today

I will . . .

- Recognize that the aging process may have some great surprises hidden within.

- Adjust to new realities. I will not worry about life's surprises—good or bad.

- Cheer myself on. I will not dwell on regrets and I will not fear failure.

- Set some goals. With God's help I will reach those goals.

- Relax, be myself, and enjoy God's wonderful peace.

Encouragement from Scripture

Lamentations 3:22–24: "Because of the Lord's great love we are not consumed, for his compassions never fail. They are new every morning; great is your faithfulness. I say to myself, 'The LORD is my portion; therefore I will wait for him.'"

Psalm 36:5: "Your love, O LORD, reaches to the heavens, your faithfulness to the skies."

Psalm 10:17–18: "You O LORD, hear the desires of the afflicted; you encourage them, and you listen to their cry, defending the fatherless and the oppressed, in order that man, who is of the earth, may terrify no more."

Jeremiah 29:13: "'You will seek me and find me when you seek me with all your heart. I will be found by you,' declares the Lord."

2 Corinthians 1:20: "For no matter how many promises God has made, they are 'Yes' in Christ. And so through Him the 'Amen' is spoken by us to the glory of God."

My prayer: I claim your steadfast faithfulness for my life today and I give You thanks.

Today with God's help—I will reflect on aspects of God's faithfulness.

A Time for Everything

What better summarization of perspective and balance than provided by Solomon:

> There is a time for everything, and a season for every activity under heaven:
> a time to be born and a time to die,
> a time to plant and a time to uproot,
> a time to kill and a time to heal,
> a time to tear down and a time to build,
> a time to weep and a time to laugh,
> a time to mourn and a time to dance,
> a time to scatter stones and a time to gather them,
> a time to embrace and a time to refrain,
> a time to search and a time to give up,
> a time to keep and a time to throw away,
> a time to tear and a time to mend,
> a time to be silent and a time to speak,
> a time to love and a time to hate,
> a time for war and a time for peace.
>
> What does the worker gain from his toil? I have seen the burden God has laid on men. He has made everything beautiful in its time. He has also set eternity in the hearts of men; yet they cannot fathom what God has done from beginning to end. I know that there is nothing better for men than to be happy and do good while they live. That everyone may eat and drink, and find satisfaction in all his toil—this is the gift of God. I know that everything God does will endure forever; nothing can be added to it and nothing taken from it. God does it so that men will revere him. (Eccl 3:1–14)

3

Enjoy Midlife

Brothers and sisters, I do not consider myself yet to
have taken hold of it. But one thing I do: Forgetting
what is behind and straining toward what is ahead, I
press on toward the goal to win the prize for which God
has called me heavenward in Christ Jesus. All of us who
are mature should take such a view of things. And if
on some point you think differently, that too God will
make clear to you. Only let us live up to what we have
already attained. (Phil 3:13-16)

A person's steps are directed by the LORD. How then
can anyone understand his own way? (Prov 20:24)

PREPARING FOR THE EMPTY NEST

EXCITEMENT FILLED the house as our son packed his
things and was off to the university. It was an exciting
time but my feelings caught me off guard one night. My wife
was asleep and I couldn't stop thinking and wondering about
how quickly the years had slipped away. I got out of bed and
quietly walked down the hallway to our son's room. I quietly
walked into that empty room and sat on the floor gazing at
an old soccer ball, an old baseball bat and glove, some large

posters on the wall, and various personal items he had left while away at school.

As you age your emotions may catch you off guard after your child drives away. You wonder how the years slipped away so quickly. You and your spouse step into your child's room, sit on the bed, and reminisce. At that moment, you realize life has changed forever—you've entered what's called the empty nest.

The empty nest means that some major components of your life and your marriage have changed. After years of parenting as your highest priority, you now find yourselves in a house alone. How you adapt will determine the success or failure of going through this transition. Talk through the following questions with your spouse:

1. How do we feel about our children being "on their own"?

2. How will we use our time now that our children are gone?

3. How will we each view our marriage now that we are alone?

4. How can we work at making our marriage stronger in this new stage of life?

5. How will we develop a new kind of intimacy now that we can focus more on each other?

As you ponder the questions, think about how meeting the following needs can help you through this difficult time:

- Reach out to people your own age and establish new friendships. Not only do you miss your children, you miss their friends. Reconnect at church, join community organizations or hobby groups, or volunteer for service projects.

- Develop new communication skills. You probably joked about sending kids on their way and enjoying the peace and quiet, but, an empty house offers deafening silence if you don't reestablish good communication with your spouse. Seek out things to talk about—join a book discussion group, invite a group of friends over to watch an uplifting movie and discuss it afterward, or reminisce about your dating and early marriage years before the kids came along.

- Develop new spiritual intimacy. Try a new approach to worship, spend time serving the Lord together inside and outside of your church, and spend quality time together.

- Learn more about each other. Again, you need to talk. Share the qualities you most admire in your spouse. What words do you love to hear your spouse say to you? When did you feel the most supported by your spouse? How can you resurrect some of those favorite moments?

- Cherish each day as a gift from God. You'll naturally cherish the days when your children were young and when they moved through adolescence and into adulthood. And perhaps someday you'll be blessed with the joy of grandchildren or even great-grandchildren. But you can learn to cherish "now" as a gift from God, too.

RETIREMENT AND BEYOND

As you approach the middle age years, it becomes increasingly important that you take specific steps to plan your future. Turning your dream for your future into reality involves formulating a plan. My goal for this chapter is to alert you that procrastination is the thief of your good intentions and that there is no substitute for solid preparation of your future.

Our financial planner was growing weary from all of my questions. Year after year I would send him emails and make telephone calls with questions about whether we would be able to survive financially if and when I made that big decision. Then I did it. I took the big plunge and told him that I was setting the date. He guided us step by step in a gracious way to lead us into that new season of life called retirement. Fortunately he knew me and knew that I would not be one to sit back and pull weeds from the yard all day. He encouraged me to think of something that I love to do and then do that part-time. Since I had been a pastor for many years I was thinking of interim work in a local church without a pastor, and even took the special training necessary for that type of work. But just before my big transition day I received a telephone call from the president of a premier conference center in Wisconsin. He told me that I could serve at the conference grounds during their peak season and return to Arizona during the winter months. I could not resist—I have found real fulfillment in retirement.

Retirement is a major transition in life and will inevitably put a great deal of stress on your marriage. Even after years of planning, this transition can come early or late. Sometimes it's the culmination of a long-awaited goal and sometimes it's the shock of "forced" retirement.

Retirement Readiness

Before I retired my wife and I attended a "Retirement Life Planning Workshop" at The Center for Ministry in Oakland,

California. During the one-day seminar we filled out and discussed a few questionnaires that proved quite helpful. For example, we filled out a "Should You Retire?" form[1]:

Circle the appropriate score.   *Score*

Do you look forward to going to your work each day?				
Never		Sometimes		Always
1	2	3	4	5

If you retired, would you miss your work associates?				
Not at all		Some		Yes
1	2	3	4	5

Do you find your work enjoyable?				
Not at all		Some		Yes
1	2	3	4	5

Does your work interfere with your personal life?				
Always		Sometimes		Never
1	2	3	4	5

Are you able to take at least several weeks of vacation each year?				
Yes		Sometimes		Always
1	2	3	4	5

Do you find yourself daydreaming about walking away from your job?				
Yes		Sometimes		Never
1	2	3	4	5

1. This questionnaire and its scoring were taken from Veninga, *Your Renaissance Years*, 10–20.

Do your family/relatives think you should retire and get away from the pressure?				
Yes		Some		No
1	2	3	4	5

Do you feel challenged by the nature of your work?				
No		Sometimes		Yes
1	2	3	4	5

Do you like the idea of earning additional money before you retire?				
No		Somewhat		Yes
1	2	3	4	5

Do you feel physically and mentally fit?				
No		Somewhat		Yes
1	2	3	4	5

Scoring: _____

If your total score is between 35 and 50, you may want to delay your retirement: your answers suggest that work provides you with considerable happiness and fulfillment. While there may be frustrations, the rewards outweigh the deficits by a significant margin. Consider putting retirement plans on hold unless you have a firm plan as to how you want to spend the next five years of your life.

If you score between 20 and 34, you should assertively plan for your future. While your job provides important benefits, there is a current of unrest that makes retirement—particularly an early retirement—appealing. A good goal to establish is that twelve months from now you will be retired or if you can't afford retirement, you will have located a new employer or type of employment.

If you score between 10 and 19, it is time to move on with your life. Do not act rashly by submitting a letter of resignation, but if you can swing it financially, set a firm day by which to begin a new era in your life. A good goal for you is to expect that in six months you will either be retired or have located a job that better fits your talents and abilities.

You may find after taking this test that work plays a more important role in your life than you thought. But you may also discover that it is time to find a new challenge.

The next exercise will help you further evaluate your emotions and preparedness for your approaching retirement.[2]

Circle the number that currently best describes your current position on the continuum.

I am _____ to face retirement					
Reluctant					Eager
1	2	3	4	5	6

I am considering retiring _____					
Under pressure					By choice
1	2	3	4	5	6

Financially, I feel _____ to retire					
Unprepared					Prepared
1	2	3	4	5	6

Emotionally, I feel _____ to retire					
Unprepared					Prepared
1	2	3	4	5	6

2. This worksheet and its scoring were provided by The Center for Ministry, Oakland, California.

I feel _____ about what retirement is apt to be like					
Pessimistic					Optimistic
1	2	3	4	5	6

I am clarifying the shape and tone of my retirement living _____					
After the fact					Well ahead
1	2	3	4	5	6

Results of this survey are meant for personal reflection or to be discussed with others. Note whether most of your responses lean toward reluctance or eagerness to retire.

Reflections on Retirement

Many feelings and thoughts are connected with the notion of retirement. The following sentence stems will help you to get in touch with your inner world.[3] Take time to complete the following:

1. I never thought I'd see the day . . .

2. The biggest challenge retirement poses . . .

3. The best part of retirement is . . .

4. I find it hard to think of letting go of . . .

5. I plan on starting . . .

6. Most people I know have retired . . .

7. My friends think in retirement I will . . .

8. The most frightening part of retirement is . . .

9. My family thinks . . .

3. Ibid.

Answering the nine open-ended statements offers an opportunity to write your personal feelings about retirement and then to reflect upon them.

Attitude Toward Retirement

On the continuum below, place an X on the line indicating your current attitude regarding retirement. At the far left is reluctance; at the far right is eagerness. Indicate your spouse's attitude with an S. Then in the columns below, list the factors on both sides that are affecting your attitude positively and negatively.[4]

Reluctant	Eager
Factors affecting Reluctance	Factors affecting Eagerness

There is no scoring of this exercise; it is meant to help you identify the factors and feelings to consider before retiring. By the time you retire, your needs and desires are quite different than they were in earlier stages of life. Like most people, you probably look forward to your retirement years, when you can pursue new opportunities, travel, do everything you put off earlier in life, and simplify your daily routine so that you can enjoy life to its fullest.

Retirement also has its stresses. Whether you liked your job or not, it gave you a sense of who you are and how you fit

4. Ibid.

into society. In a culture that identifies people by what they do, retirement can make you feel like you've been stripped of your worth. The routine, the familiar pressures, the fun of accomplishing tasks, and the comradeship with coworkers are all gone.

Although many retirees remain active and independent, they desire a simpler lifestyle with less responsibilities and more social activities. Today's retirees enjoy not just motor homes and travel, but also motorcycling, rock climbing, in-line skating, or dancing.

Expand Your View of Retirement

How will you deal with your retirement years? These ideas can help you along the way:

- Change how you think of retirement. I think of it as a transition! This is the time to set new goals and challenges, things you only dreamed about in the past.

- Find an identity separate from your former work. Think of all those projects you put off, the trips you want to take, hobbies you love, time with family, kids, and grandkids. Dream my friend, dream and enjoy.

- Renew relationships with friends. You and your spouse can spend time with people you haven't seen for years.

PREPARING FOR GRANDKIDS AND BEYOND

My wife and I had the amazing opportunity to be in the birthing room during the birth of both of our granddaughters. I remember when our son was born, poor old Dad sat for hours all alone in the hospital waiting room and then shortly after 3:17 a.m. I received only a glance at him as I peeked through a glass window into the nursery. A couple of years later when our daughter was born I watched on a monitor in a private father's waiting room. Today, mothers may invite selected family members to be right in the birthing room with her. So nine years ago and again seven years ago, my wife and I stood next to our daughter and her husband as she gave birth to our granddaughters. What a thrill that was. Our daughter had assigned each of us specific responsibilities. Her husband was to be her encourager and to cut the umbilical cord. I was to discretely videotape the delivery. Grandma was to be her aide and provide general help as needed. When the time came for cutting the umbilical cord Dad was so emotional that Grandma had to do the honors (and Grandpa was very discrete in videotaping).

Being a grandparent is one of the greatest thrills in life. Stories are endless, but I just cannot resist two more silly stories about grandchildren and grandparents.

I read a story about Grandpa walking his grandson to the elementary school playground. When they arrived Grandpa noticed one of the children making faces at others on the playground. Grandpa gently reproved the child. Smiling sweetly, Grandpa said, "When I was a child, I was told if I made ugly faces, it would freeze and I would stay like that." The child looked up and innocently replied, "Well, you can't say you weren't warned."

A boy had reached age four without giving up the habit of sucking his thumb, though his mother had tried everything from bribery to reasoning to painting it with lemon juice to discourage the habit. One night the boy stayed overnight at Grandma and Grandpa's house. Grandma had the perfect warning, "If you don't stop sucking your thumb, your stomach is going to blow up like a balloon." The next day when the boy was with his mom, as they were walking down the sidewalk, mother and son saw a pregnant woman sitting in the front yard on a swing. The four-year-old considered her gravely for a minute, then spoke to her saying, "Uh oh . . . I know what you've been doing."

And finally the joke that brings a grin to grown-up faces. A certain little girl, when asked her name, would reply, "I'm Mr. Brown's daughter." Her grandmother told her that was not correct, she should say, "I'm Jane Brown." The pastor spoke to her Sunday school class and said, "Aren't you Mr. Brown's daughter?" She replied, "I thought I was, but my grandma says I'm not."

We love our grandchildren so much and often see and hear the strangest things. If you are younger and don't have grandchildren or older and not blessed with grandchildren, you probably think of marriage in the present. When your children are grown and God blesses you with grandchildren and perhaps great-grandchildren, how will that affect your marriage in the years ahead?

There is nothing quite like seeing grandchildren come into this world. As we watch our two granddaughters grow, we see personalities forming. On occasion when they spend the night with Grandma and Grandpa, late at night I slip down the hall and see them sleeping on our living room couch. One evening when their mom and dad were "out on a date," I looked at their innocent faces and memories of years gone by flooded my mind. Grandparenting is quite the "season of life."

As grandparents or great-grandparents, we have the joy of being with the children and then with a grin, we hand them back to Mom and Dad. Many grandparents joke, "We spoil them and give them back." Being a grandparent or great-grandparent is one of the greatest thrills in life.

Psalm 78:4 reminds us that it is a joy and privilege to "tell the next generation the praiseworthy deeds of the Lord, His power, and the wonders He has done." If you have grandkids or great grandkids, consider these four questions:

1. What positive actions and attitudes do I display to help nurture my grandchildren and great-grandchildren in spiritual things?

2. How can I share my family history—both joys and sorrows— in a positive way?

3. What will I need to do to mentor my grandchildren and great-grandchildren?

4. What values do my grandchildren and great-grandchildren see in me? How can I strengthen those values in their lives?

Grandparenting takes a team effort. Your lifestyle permits your grandchildren and great-grandchildren to "see in action" what a biblically sound, godly life is like. If your marriage is God honoring, you can share God's love with your grandchildren. Try the following five practical tips for communicating your love:

1. Accept your grandchildren for who they are. Respect each grandchild as a special person. Discover something unique about each grandchild and provide an opportunity to encourage his or her development. Believe in your grandchildren. Never ridicule them, and compliment them often.

2. Take time to be with your grandchildren. Plan a day together to just have fun. Go hiking, fishing, camping, or plan a trip to a park. Spend time together having fun. Even if you live far away, plan some special times with and for grandchildren when you do get together.

3. Do activities together. Prepare a meal. Bake a cake or brownies together. Go grocery shopping and let your grandkids choose some foods. Young children love to scramble eggs, plus they get to enjoy a good breakfast after the work is done!

4. Be patient, fair, consistent, firm, and forgiving. Children have an amazing way of moving on without holding grudges. They respect discipline and learn great lessons.

5. Show affection to each grandchild. Give them lot of hugs and kisses. Be sure you're modeling a loving marriage so they will see this love relationship and grow to love and respect others. Learn to communicate with your grandchildren. Sharpen your computer skills and take advantage of email, text messaging, Facebook, Skype, Web 2.0, or whatever technological advances help you to stay in touch with your grandchildren.[5]

Growing Your Trust in God

Find a quiet spot where you can be alone for a brief time and take a few moments to read Psalm 78. To personalize the scripture, respond to the following five questions:

1. What are the praiseworthy deeds of the Lord?

2. What were the reasons behind the Israelites' chronic lack of faith?

3. How did God respond to the failures of the Israelites?

4. What are the wonders God has done in my own life?

5. Why is it that I fail to trust God despite evidence of his goodness and power?

5. Gutowski, *Grandparents Are Forever*, 38–39.

PURSUING NEW INTERESTS

Each of us has different interests. My wife loves handicrafts, playing the piano, reading, and stitchery. I enjoy active activities like hiking and bicycle riding. As we age we must guard against trying to make our spouse more like we are. I did that for a number of years and found it to be destructive. If you are highly organized and your spouse is quite relaxed, flexible, and unorganized, enjoy your differences and accept the fact that God made you each unique. You each benefit from the other. It would definitely not be good if everyone were the same. God made each of us special. We each need to cultivate the interests we have. We should use our talents and gifts and keep growing as individuals.

An important key for keeping your long-term marriage alive is clear and simple communication. You and your spouse need to communicate not just your thoughts and ideas, but also your feelings. Try using "I" messages and reflective listening:

- "I" messages state the effect on you: "I feel [name the emotion]."
- Reflective listening states what you heard your spouse say: "What I understand you saying is that you are feeling . . . because . . . "

Another important element to keeping long-term marriages alive is doing new things together. Try these ideas to help cultivate new interests:

- Help beautify the church (inside or outside)
- Volunteer at a local hospital or hospice
- Help as a team in Sunday school, small group, children's ministry, youth ministry, or young adult ministry

- Volunteer as a couple at a skilled nursing care or assisted living center
- Offer your services at the library, sports arena, Little League, and so on
- Provide transportation, prepare meals, and/or take food to the homebound
- Call members of your church on their birthday or anniversary
- Help in a local school or after school program
- Volunteer at the American Red Cross, YMCA, or YWCA

As you get out and start to do things as a retired individual or couple, there will also be new opportunities to make friends. Now is a good time to ask yourself: Who do I/we feel comfortable with as we try to make new friends?

Understanding New Roles

After leaving full-time ministry and transitioning into retirement, our various roles and responsibilities have changed. I no longer come home from the office. When I began my part-time staff position at Green Lake Conference Center in Wisconsin, I was no longer the lead pastor of a growing church. I had much more time and could assume much more responsibility at home. We established a new plan for meals, cleaning, dishes, and other household chores. We do not have a dishwasher in the small apartment at the conference center and that gave us a wonderful opportunity to wash and dry dishes together. We shared more and more responsibilities and found new meaning in our relationship. One night I was thinking of that old Beatles song, "will you still need me, will you still love me, when I'm sixty-four?" We found that not only life, but also marriage itself is a cycle. We began with just the two of us. Then our son came along and then our daughter. The years passed by quickly and then we found ourselves back to just the two of us.

Keeping long-term marriages alive by understanding new roles will involve facing some new realities:

- We've both changed through the years and we need to work hard at communicating our feelings as equals.

- We must both make a new commitment to absolute faithfulness to one another and to God.

- We both need to evaluate our use of time. Now that we have more time, how will we use it and what will we do together?

- We both must accept the fact that we need to spend time together in reading scripture, in prayer, and in worship with the family of God.

With these thoughts in mind, approach your pastor about offering a preaching series not just on marriage enrichment for young couples, but on marriage enrichment for later-in-life marriages as well. Your pastor can help later-in-life couples answer the following questions:

1. How can we develop new intimacy with each other?

2. What new roles do we have during this time and stage of marriage and what do we each need to do to function happily in our new roles?

3. How have friendships changed and what family members and friends have moved away?

4

Prepare for the Later Years

The righteous will flourish like a palm tree, they will grow like a cedar of Lebanon; planted in the house of the LORD, they will flourish in the courts of our God. They will still bear fruit in old age, they will stay fresh and green, proclaiming, "The LORD is upright; he is my Rock, and there is no wickedness in him." (Ps 92:12–15)

The glory of young men is their strength, gray hair the splendor of the old. (Prov 20:29)

PREPARING FOR NEW USES OF TIME

IT ISN'T true that as we age we become more like everyone else. I have found, in fact, that as people mature they become even more unique and individualistic. It's also a myth to think that older adults contribute less as they age. People in retirement years volunteer more than any other age segment.[1]

---

1. In my years of working with people age fifty and "better," I have found this to be true. This data is also supported by Sweeting, *Joys of Successful Aging*, 49; Storm, *Second Half Adventure*, 29; Hanson, *Baby Boomers and Beyond*, 28; and Del Webb's video, "Redefining Retirement."

Today older adults live longer, are more active, and are more creative than ever before. Almost one quarter of the average American's life is spent in retirement. Today's older adults have a new face—the face of volunteerism.

As people mature past middle adulthood and into older adulthood, there are significant differences compared to older adults of years past. In years past, older adults were thought of as care receivers; today they are caregivers. Many older adults that I know are involved in a care-giving ministry. They volunteer at local hospitals, service organizations, and in the church. Some are volunteers at hospice, others at the library. Most older adults enjoy being helpful, they enjoy being involved, and they enjoy staying active.

Older adults want to see results of their efforts. In the past, many churches across America gave little attention to older adult ministry. If we are to grow spiritually and follow Christ's command, churches will need to place a major focus on middle age and older adult ministry. Outdated stereotypes of seniors will have to be discarded and new images of active, vibrant, mature adults must come into focus. Intergenerational activities are helpful as well.

I heard the funny story about an elderly man who had serious hearing problems for a number of years. He went to the doctor and the doctor was able to have him fitted for a set of hearing aids that allowed the gentleman to hear 100 percent. The elderly man went back in a month to the doctor and the doctor said, "Your hearing is perfect. Your family must be really pleased that you can hear again." The gentleman replied, "Oh, I haven't told my family just yet. I just sit around and listen to the conversations. I've changed my will three times."

Aging successfully involves staying active, being with family as much as possible, and mixing intergenerationally. Mixing intergenerationally is certainly not without its challenges.

There was a woman who was visiting a church one Sunday morning. The sermon seemed to go on forever and many in the congregation fell asleep. After the service, to be social, she walked up to a very sleepy looking elderly man, extended her hand in greeting, and said, "Hello, I'm Gladys Dunn." The man replied, "You're not the only one ma'am, I'm glad it's done too!"

Learning to live with who we are and what we have is an important lesson in aging successfully. Older adults today have amazing opportunities for outreach to help others. Your church might have a drama team without actors, small groups without leaders, or a library without librarians. Why not jump in and help? By volunteering, you not only provide service, but if you are married, you strengthen your relationship as you serve the Lord together.

The list of ways you can serve is almost limitless. Tap into your interests. For example, if you love to travel, serve on a short-term mission trip.

Volunteer—Move from Sitting to Serving

What skills do you have? What are you passionate about? What experiences have you had that might help you help others? Here are some other ways you can serve independently or together:

- Small group leaders
- Pastoral assistance
- Home repair
- Church library

- Kitchen and cooking
- Cleaning and yard work for the homebound who need assistance
- Financial planning (provided by those who have such ministry gifts)
- Missions and outreach
- Music and drama
- Worship leaders
- Tele-Care ministry (calling people in need of services or friendship)
- Prison ministry
- Tutoring

Changing Energy and Interest

So, how's your sense of humor? Humor is wonderful. I often enjoy sharing a good joke before I make a presentation at a conference or before I begin my teaching. The Bible says that laughter is good medicine (Ps 126:2; Prov 15:13, 15; 17:22). You may have heard these four humorous statements about aging

- Seen it all, done it all, can't remember most of it. In dog years—I'm dead.
- Brain cells come and go, but fat cells live forever.
- He's reached the age where they only put four or five candles on his birthday cake. One for each tooth.
- The real reason old men date younger women is they need someone who can drive at night.

Many of us grew up eating fast food and living a fast-paced life. In the early years of adulthood you may have eaten junk food, drank jumbo-sized sugar-filled drinks, and might not have been all that active. It's never too late to start eating healthy, drinking more water, and exercising. As you age and your energy and interests change, you face new challenges and new opportunities. The apostle Paul wrote that our bodies are the temple of the Holy Spirit (see 1 Cor 6:19).

No matter how old you are, *now* is a great time to face the challenge and get healthier. Most people know academically the simple keys to a healthier lifestyle, but it takes motivation. If you are married, why not set that goal together, holding each other accountable for living healthier?

As I think of preparing for changing energy and interests, I think back over the years and see changes in my life. There were not only changes in energy and interest but physical, mental, emotional, social, and spiritual changes that are all part of the maturing process. Our particular denomination strongly suggests that their pastors go to a counseling center at the beginning, middle, and just before the conclusion of their lifelong ministry. So forty years ago my wife and I went off to their counseling center to evaluate our communication skills, marriage, goals, and so forth. I kept the printout from the various inventories from forty years ago. About twenty years ago we went back and found that our goals had drastically changed as did our ministry styles. We attended that career counseling center one last time just before retirement and looked back at forty years of ministry together. It was fascinating to look at our marriage, our parenting, our ministry, and our goals and to see how we had grown together. It sort of provided a snapshot of who we were over the years and where we would be in the coming years. We saw how the word accountability had become important: accountability to one another and to our family, accountability to our church family, and accountability to God.

Accountability Statements

Here are some accountability statements to get you started. We will be accountable to each other as we . . .

- Eat healthier and maintain our proper weight.

- Exercise either on a personal program, as a couple, or in a group setting.

- Work on getting enough rest.

- Drink plenty of water and balance our work and our play.

- Participate faithfully worship, the study of God's Word, and service for the Lord.

- Take a proactive, not passive, approach to assume a sense of responsibility for our own health.

- Learn to manage stress and conflict in our marriage.

- Learn to grow in a circle of Christian friends and establish relationships for love and caring for one another.[2]

NEW AND DIFFERENT IDEA OF WHAT LOVE MEANS

As we approached another wedding anniversary, I was trying to think of something creative. What can you do that is different after over thirty years of marriage? I wanted our wedding anniversary to be a surprise. I telephoned the Hyatt hotel in downtown Phoenix and made a one-night room reservation. On our anniversary day I suggested to my wife that we just go walk around downtown and keep this anniversary simple. She asked if we would go out for dinner and if so,

2. Contributions to this list were made by Jerry and Shirley Rose, *GPS God's Plan for Significance*, 106–7.

how should she dress? I encouraged her to just be flexible and not worry. I told her we could just decide at the moment and to just dress comfortably.

Unbeknown to her I packed an overnight bag for the two of us and set it in the trunk of the car. When we arrived downtown, we walked around a shopping area and of course she wanted to look in some specialty shops, which gave me the perfect opportunity to suggest she shop and we meet at a given point in an hour—which we did. While she was window-shopping in specialty shops I quickly raced to the car, pulled out the overnight bag, and raced to the Hyatt to check in. Next I rushed up to the twenty-first floor, put her clothes in the dresser, put a rose on the table along with a card, and set a few mints on her pillow. Then I dashed back down to where we were to meet and greeted her unassumingly.

I suggested that we walk over to the Hyatt and perhaps just take the elevator to the top floor to enjoy a view of the city. When we entered the elevator, I pushed the button for the twenty-first floor. When the doors opened, she realized that we had not reached the top floor, to which I suggested that we just walk up the extra flight. As we walked down the hallway heading for the stairway, we came to the room I had reserved. I pulled the door key from my pocket and slipped it into the door lock and we walked in. You can imagine her surprise when she saw her personal items, the flower, and mints. Of course she was thrilled and that simple creative event reminded us both of our wonderful marriage of over thirty years together.

Maybe you're acquainted with the various Greek words for love. The three most common are *eros*, *philia*, and *agape*. Love is about far more than sex. Later-in-life couples can make sure their expressions of love for each other are well-rounded, encompassing all that these three words mean.

Eros is the love that seeks sensual expression—romantic love and sexual love. It's inspired by the biological part of human nature. In a strong marriage, you'll love each other romantically and erotically. Yet in later-in-life marriages, sexual challenges can arise. So if your marriage has been built only on eros, you could be in trouble.

If your marriage is strong, you and your spouse are also good friends. Friendship means companionship, communication, and cooperation. That's philia love—true friends who enjoy each other.

Then there's agape love. Agape is the self-giving love. It's the love that goes on loving even when the other person is unloving. This sort of love doesn't come naturally. You and your spouse must work at making this kind of love a part of your marriage.

Love in your later-in-life marriage will suffer if you and your spouse don't have a clear understanding of these three biblical concepts of love. In addition, you must be willing to communicate deeply and have an absolute commitment to each other. If you and your spouse suddenly declare that you no longer love each other, the real question is, "When did you choose to *not* love one another?"

What kills love? Love dies when you spend little or no time together and when you stop sharing activities that are mutually enjoyable. You create or destroy love by deciding to or not to have pleasurable activities (not necessarily sex) over a period of time together. Your marriage relationship diminishes when either you or your spouse (or both of you) stop smiling, caressing, complimenting, showing compassion, and spending time together.

Facing Marital Challenges

Marriage relationships can be rewarding but they can also present challenges. When difficulties surface there are many things we can do to improve this special relationship. Here are some questions to discuss if you're currently facing marital challenges:

1. What do you do to reinforce the behaviors you enjoy?

2. What can you do to increase feelings of friendship and deepen the love relationship with your spouse?

3. How can the presence of Jesus in your life help you love your spouse through eros, philia, and agape love?

PREPARING FOR SERIOUS ILLNESS

My associate's wife had leukemia. Over the years I'd watched their relationship closely. They had been married for over fifty years. They were very close and had given many testimonies of God's goodness. But the roller coaster of good news and bad news had been a tremendous challenge. She was in and out of the hospital and back and forth to specialists and emergency rooms. Finally the day came. I had been visiting her in the hospital nearly every day, but her life was now slipping away quickly. That night she breathed her last breath and with family around the bedside, we sang and prayed and reflected about an amazing lady who was now in heaven.

If you or your spouse is facing serious illness, these reminders can bring hope and comfort:

- Find someone to talk to about the illness. Talking is one of the best ways to face feelings. You might think it's too difficult to talk about deep hurts, but it's far more difficult to experience the hurt and not talk.

- Accept the realities of aging. While it can be tough

to face the reality of aging and its challenges, make a conscious effort to find its joys as well.

- Look at each day as a gift from God. Focus on the positive as much as you can. God can put a song in your heart even if you or your spouse is lying on a bed in a hospital room or sitting in a wheelchair at home.

- Remember that all life is fragile. You have this moment in time and the future is in God's hands. That truth hasn't changed during your whole lifetime! Try to thank God for the blessings you've enjoyed over the many years you've had together as a couple.

- Experience the power of prayer. Prayer is powerful. Just talk to God. The Holy Spirit dwells in believers, providing comfort. Jesus promised, "I will ask the Father, and he will give you another Counselor to be with you forever—the Spirit of truth" (John 14:16–17).

- Keep on keeping on. Ultimately, you'll learn to comfort yourself. No matter how many people are around someone with a serious illness during the day, reality can be tough to face in the loneliness of night. You must learn to cheer yourself to move forward with God's help.

- Set goals for yourself. No matter how small, any goal can help you feel a sense of achievement. For example, if you're healing from hip surgery, those first five steps with a walker are huge accomplishments.

- Keep a sense of humor. Learn to laugh at yourself and the funny things around you. See humor and laugher as gifts God provides to offer relief from your difficult times.

Remember the simple words of Solomon: "A cheerful heart is good medicine, but a broken spirit saps a person's strength" (Prov 17:22).

- Be thankful for each day and greet it joyously. God is the giver of joy.

- Accept comfort offered by friends and family. The strong support of all the people who love you might be the strongest medicine.

- Claim God's strength and fill your heart with scripture's promises. Meditate on verses and passages such as Psalm 119; Romans 5:3; 8:28; 11:33–36; 1 Corinthians 10:13; and James 1:12.

Sometimes sharing feelings is important. Sometimes just being quiet and letting God speak is even more important.

PREPARING FOR NEW OPPORTUNITIES AND CHANGE

Being together as a couple for the long haul offers many wonderful and new opportunities. Time together has a way of offering both challenges and amazing opportunities for growth. As a couple, you just need to learn your new roles and how to communication well.

You also have a new relationship with your children during these times. While your children have moved on into careers, they can share with you meaningful things going on in their work and family life. Often children seek their parents' counsel about parenting. Amazing doors of opportunity can open as you share your wisdom and experience.

New opportunities can arise in other areas as well. Here are some simple and practical suggestions to help you enjoy new opportunities together:

- Keep your faith strong by maintaining a fresh, personal, vibrant relationship with God.

- Maintain godly character traits through constant evaluation and dialogue with your spouse since he or she sees your blind spots.

- Be faithful in worship and fellowship at your church because worshipping together has amazing power to draw two people together.

- Get involved in a good small group for accountability and support.

- Live a godly life through obeying the commands in scripture.

- Serve the Lord together by working together in helping others. For example, consider mentoring a younger married couple.

SUCCESSFUL RELATIONSHIPS

Couples in later-in-life marriages who are successful in their relationships generally display these four characteristics:

1. They set priorities together and work hard at putting God first and each other second, followed by the many pressing needs and pressures of life.

2. They balance their lives with a good blend of time for each other and time together with mutual friends.

3. They keep a close watch for signs of their marriage relationship slipping, by observing any nagging, sarcasm, communication breakdown, or jealousy.

4. They develop their own areas for using spiritual gifts and help their spouse develop his or her spiritual giftedness.

Do the qualities above describe your marriage? If not, what can you do to claim them? After considering the four items above, it's time to evaluate how you feel you are doing in each area to prepare for your future. This involves change and change involves risk, insecurity, and vulnerability. My wife and I began thinking and praying together about the opportunity at Green Lake Conference Center. It was extremely important that we do a lot of evaluating and reflecting. This needed to be something we would both be happy with. As it turns out, when we spent our first summer at Green Lake she began to volunteer at the craft center located on the grounds. She was helping others and loving every minute of it.

I have found that in order to make a change successfully, there are five things you should be sure of. First, be sure the change meets a need. If change is simply for change's sake, most people will not readily accept or adjust to the change. Your children or grandchildren may think you need to move closer to them or into an assisted living center. Openness to change will come only as *you* sense a need for the change. Your spouse may have a very different idea about change. We are all so unique.

Second, be sure your spouse is in agreement, joins you in feeling the need for change, and understands the potential consequences. You and your spouse will need to do a lot of communicating as you continue to grow together. Consensus is the goal; when you both know you are ready for the change—move ahead. To make positive change, we must understand and accept the consequences for others as well as ourselves.

Third, make sure you believe that the change can be accomplished. This may take time. It's one thing to demonstrate a need; it is quite another to show that the change can be accomplished. Praying together and planning together are critical. "Baby steps" become important. Begin with what you *can* do, and then gradually move on to the bigger steps that will be a challenge.

Fourth, make sure that you believe the change is better than what you already have. If things are comfortable now, why change? That seems logical to anyone. It's important to discuss reasons why the change is needed. This does not happen overnight.

Finally, make sure your spouse is involved in the entire process of change. Simply making the change, and then announcing it, will create havoc and incur bad feelings. Involving your spouse, children, and grandchildren in the process and allowing adequate time for adjustment will bring lasting results.

5

Focus on the Biblical View

Gray hair is a crown of splendor; it is attained by a righteous life. (Prov 16:31)

BIBLICAL AND SPIRITUAL ISSUES OF AGING

OUR TWENTY-FIRST-CENTURY society has a very different view of aging than what the Bible has. It is important to understand God's view of successful aging. The goal of this chapter is to provide a biblical framework for aging. What is your image of aging and how does that impact your life? Numerous Bible passages are given that can encourage us.

Many denominations have small churches filled with older people, and many other churches have changed their focus to reach today's younger culture. Some pastors are confused and frustrated by this change, and many longtime church members find the shift frustrating. Older pastors find it difficult to understand contemporary styles of worship, and younger pastors sometimes move very quickly toward creating what they understand to be necessary changes within the congregation. The results can often cause frustration and even be hurtful for many.

With all of this change comes an important question: "What is our image of aging?" In the past, the aged were an integral part of family and community life. A substantial pattern of social disengagement and isolation emerged during the middle of the twentieth century. The farm and agricultural culture was replaced with urban renewal, and the family unit changed. Grandma and Grandpa no longer had children close by to help during times of need. Social workers began to take the place of children and family, and care centers replaced home care.

Because of these factors, isolation has become a major issue for older adults. With family gone, the church becomes even more important in providing loving and caring support. Imagine how an older adult would feel if he or she began to see their church changing dramatically and found they are being passed by or excluded. The issue of isolation becomes even more intensified.

Some older adults are going through major losses in physical and mental functioning as well. Many have lost their spouse, many have seen their children move away, and many have felt that their church has become very different, a foreign place where once they felt at home. Now they feel unwanted, displaced, and perhaps even unwelcome.

We live in a society that is quick to label people and groups. As attention has been drawn to aging, the idea has developed to label some adults as "old" and sometimes even to make them feel "unneeded" or "in the way."

Most of us have stereotypes of older adults just sitting back in their rocking chairs. That's a myth. Older adults are incredibly active people today with tremendous experience and resources that we all too often don't utilize. Many times that is because we hold outdated stereotypes of what aging is. I recently read about a pastor in one of America's largest churches who never talked about older adults until he turned fifty. Then he began to realize the importance of this neglected ministry. It makes perfect sense. A pastor who has never been married may have a hard time understanding the gut-wrenching conflicts faced in some marriages. A thirty-year-old pastor may find it even uncomfortable to be with seventy- or eighty-year-olds. But it is time for pastors to dump the old stereotypes and catch up; mix with and get to know some elderly folks. I was in a contemporary worship service a while back at a very rapidly growing church of several thousand people and heard the pastor, who was middle-aged himself say, "We don't want any creepy old people coming to this new program." Everyone laughed, except the older people present who noticeably felt uncomfortable and unwanted.

Historically, Eastern cultures have shown great respect and care for the eldest among them. Not only do they read from right to left, their generational perspective appears to be flipped 180 degrees. Most churches in the Western world appear to think strategically from *youngest to oldest*. Eastern cultures think *oldest to youngest*.

Scriptural teaching on discipleship suggests it's our Western church culture that may be directionally challenged. Unfortunately, churches with a primary focus on the young will often stop far short of reaching and equipping every generation.

There are traditionally two opposite thoughts of old age in cultures around the world—a sort of continuum. At one end of the continuum cultures place a positive regard on aging. To be old is to be wise, to have high social influence, and to be deeply respected. At the other end of the cultural continuum is a negative view of aging. Old age is inherently filled with irreversible losses. To be old is to be physically incapacitated, to suffer the loss of mental capabilities, to become economically dependent, to experience social isolation, and to lose social status. Unfortunately, not only has much of America fallen into that pattern of thinking; sadly, the church has often joined this train of thought as well.

Perhaps we need to start thinking strategically from oldest-to-youngest rather than youngest-to-oldest. We need to change our vocabulary and make sure that no generation is left behind!

Someone once said, "The best way to cope with change is to help create it." We must never assume that older generations are universally resistant to change.[1] They have experienced and adapted to *incredible* changes throughout their lifetime. Welcome their input. If changes are biblically sound and God-directed, patiently cultivate and expect their support.

"Some global trends shed new light on what the future may hold for the aging in cultures where respect for them is compromised. A United Nations study conducted by the Second World Assembly on Aging looked at world population aging from 1950 through 2050 and revealed three facts:

1. Population aging is unprecedented, without parallel in the history of humanity.

2. Population aging is profound, having major consequences and implications for all facets of human life.

3. Population aging is enduring: We will not return to the young populations our ancestors knew.

Aging trends *will* dictate a new perspective."[2]

---

1. Read Gordon MacDonald's *Who Stole My Church?* for a wonderful perspective on engaging older generations in the change process.

2. "Second World Assembly on Ageing," http://www.c-fam.org/docLib /20080625_Madrid_Ageing_Conference.pdf, quoted in Lane, "Graying

Charles Arn and Win Arn in their book, *The New Senior*, share this insight, "We live in a day when racism and sexism have been recognized as the unwholesome attitudes they are. Yet, unfortunately, ageism is alive and well—even in the church. Although it is no longer considered in good taste to make racist or sexist jokes, old age is still fair game. Ageism is a pervasive, negative attitude toward aging and people who are growing old. Like racism or sexism, it is a destructive and discriminatory form of prejudice that is based on flawed stereotypes. To a large extent, ageism is unique to our contemporary Western culture. For example, in much of Asia it is seen as a handicap to be young, and ageism is virtually nonexistent. In China, it is believed that the older a person is the wiser and more knowledgeable the person is. When asked, 'How old are you?' a 55-year-old in China might fudge a bit and claim to be 60."[3]

High Regard for Aging

It doesn't take a biblical scholar to know what position the Bible takes on aging. God places a high regard on aging. Note these biblical concepts:

Old age is given as a reward: "The fear of the LORD adds length to life, but the years of the wicked are cut short" (Prov 10:27), and "And if you walk in my ways and obey my statutes and commands as David your father did, I will give you a long life" (1 Kgs 3:14).

Wisdom and understanding can come with aging: "Is not wisdom found among the aged? Does not long life bring understanding?" (Job 12:12), and "Remember the days of old; consider the generations long past. Ask your father and

around the Globe," 11 (emphasis in the original).

3. Arn and Arn, *New Senior*, 46.

he will tell you; your elders, and they will explain to you" (Deut 32:7).

God promises continued support to older persons: "Even to your old age and gray hairs I am he, I am he who will sustain you. I have made you and I will carry you; I will sustain you and I will rescue you" (Isa 46:4).

We should not lose respect for the elderly people: "Rise in the presence of the aged, show respect for the elderly and revere your God. I am the LORD" (Lev 19:32).

As we grow older, we have the ability to grow in God's Grace: "But grow in the grace and knowledge of our Lord and Savior Jesus Christ. To him be glory both now and forever! Amen" (2 Pet 3:18).

Life is filled with various "seasons," and aging gracefully is in God's plan for creation: "There is a time for everything, and a season for every activity under Heaven: a time to be born and a time to die, a time to plant and a time to uproot" (Eccl 3:1).

All persons are created in God's image: "So God created man in his own image, in the image of God he created him; male and female he created them. God blessed them and said to them, 'Be fruitful and increase in number; fill the earth and subdue it. Rule over the fish of the sea and the birds of the air and over every living creature that moves on the ground'" (Gen 1:27–28).

We are to encourage older persons and point them to the Lord for strength: "Do not cast me away when I am old; do not forsake me when my strength is gone" (Ps 71:9).

Older persons are to continue enjoying that which they have produced: "No longer will they build houses and others live in them, or plant and others eat. For as the days of a tree, so will be the days of my people; my chosen ones will long enjoy the works of their hands" (Isa 65:22).

Be gentle and respectful when talking to older persons: "Do not rebuke an older man harshly, but exhort him as if he were your father. Treat younger men as brothers, older women as mothers, and younger women as sisters, with absolute purity" (1 Tim 5:1–2).

The Bible is filled with examples of men and women who remained active servants of the Lord even in their later years. Abraham, Moses, David, and the apostle John are some of the earliest examples of older adults who remained active in serving the Lord. Intergenerational relationships become very important as well. The friendship of Paul and Timothy provides a great example of the older mentoring the younger.

Of all the biblical teaching on aging, 1 Corinthians seems to be one of the most important. The apostle Paul wrote, "The body is a unit, though it is made up of many parts; and though all its parts are many, they form one body. So it is with Christ" (1 Cor 12:12), and in verses 21–23 Paul continues, "The eye cannot say to the hand, 'I don't need you!' And the head cannot say to the feet, 'I don't need you!' On the contrary, those parts of the body that seem to be weaker are indispensable, and the parts that we think are less honorable we treat with special honor. And the parts that are unpresentable are treated with special modesty.'" Paul's message is that *every* member of the body of Christ is important—young and old.

Truth About Aging

Read the following scripture references to discover how the Bible addresses aging and longevity. In column two, briefly jot down what the verse says about aging or longevity. In column three, note your own personal response.

Focus on the Biblical View

Bible Reference	What the Bible Says About Aging	My Response
Ecclesiastes 3:1–2		
Genesis 1:27		
1 Kings 3:14		
Proverbs 10:27		
Job 12:12		
Deuteronomy 32:7		
Psalm 71:18		
Psalm 92:14		
Psalm 1:3		
Isaiah 46:4		
Psalm 71:9		
Leviticus 19:32		
1 Timothy 5:1–2		
Isaiah 65:22		
1 Corinthians 15:58		
Galatians 5:22–23		
2 Peter 3:18		

6

Understand Loss and Grief

> I remember my affliction and my wandering, the bitterness and the gall. I well remember them, and my soul is downcast within me. Yet this I call to mind and therefore I have hope: Because of the LORD's great love we are not consumed, for his compassions never fail. They are new every morning; great is your faithfulness. I say to myself, 'The LORD is my portion; therefore I will wait for him.' The LORD is good to those whose hope is in him, to the one who seeks him; it is good to wait quietly for the salvation of the LORD. (Lam 3:24–26)

DEALING WITH LOSS AND GRIEF

THERE IS a serious side to aging. Anyone who has ever worked with or known older adults knows that dealing with grief, pain, suffering, and loss is part of the territory. This is the downside of working with older adults. "'The ratio between young and old is changing, and soon the whole world will look like Florida,' observed journalist Gavin du Venage last year. He's right. A drop in infant morality, eradication of certain diseases, better medical care, and healthier diets all have helped boost longevity in the developed West to record levels."[1] According to the U. S. Census Bureau there are now 40.3 million people 65 years and older—up 15.1 percent from 2000 to 2010 and representing the fastest growing segment of the population. While the number of 65- to 74-year-olds grew 18.1 percent and 75- to 84-year-olds inched up another 5.7 percent, the number of 85- to 94-year-olds jumped a whopping 29.9 percent.[2]

It has been said that we don't "do death well." If you visit a mortuary, you'll hear staff giving happy names to sad things. You'll hear pleasant phrases like "slumber rooms" and bodies being referred to as "remains." Ashes will be called "cremains," and funeral directors will seldom even use the word *death*. Many think that if we don't talk about death, it won't happen. Older adults, however, know that death will happen. Simply put—the death rate is one each! Someone once said, "The leading cause of death is life."[3]

I recently conducted two funerals: one of a husband and then a year later, the man's wife. The wife's funeral was in the same month as her husband's. At the wife's memorial service, I shared thoughts from the poem *Wild Grapes* by Robert Frost. In that poem, Frost talks about wisdom. The first part of wisdom, according to Frost, is to learn to let go with our hands. The second is to learn what to hold on to with our heart. Oddly enough, with our fear and avoidance of death, we at the same time seem to have a fascination with death and dying. We learn early on that grief is bad and something to fear and avoid. But the Bible has a completely different view of death and grief.

---

1. Kennedy, "Senior Moment," 47.

2. "The Older Population: 2010," http://2010.census.gov/news/pdf/201111 30_slides.pdf, slides 7–12.

3. Manning, *Gift of Significance*, 5, 7.

Most people do not like to think or talk about dying. However, for believers this is a powerful time for growth. Times of crisis actually are among the most powerful times for spiritual growth.

Is There "Good Grief"?

Can grief actually be good? One of the first funerals I conducted was of a young man whose life's desire was to be a Marine. After only a week in active military service, he was shot and killed. His body was flown back to the States. I'll never forget his grieving parents as the flag was draped over the casket. Their question haunted my mind as they asked, "Why?" I have learned that through our own grief, we can become instruments of God and his grace.

Five Good Things Hidden in Grief

Grief can be good when we . . .

- Understand that our feelings and our timelines differ.
- Realize that the stages of grieving often blend and merge together.
- Remember that God is always with us and covers us.
- Let it open a door of opportunity to help someone else.
- Let our heart help to readjust our priorities and focus on God.

There is good in our grief when we understand that our feelings and timelines of moving through the grief process differ greatly. Psalm 91:1 reminds us that "he who dwells in the shelter of the Most High will *rest* in the shadow of the Almighty." Learning to rest in the shadow of the Almighty is not easy. For some people that comes quickly, but for others it may take years. People respond to grief in different ways and on different timelines. Grief can be something as horrible as a catastrophe, such as the loss of a spouse, child, grandchild, or close friend. Grief can also be experienced when we're in a financial crisis, moving to a new community, having to make new friends, or having disappointments in our lives because our children or grandchildren did not go in the direction we prayed they would. Death, divorce, marital separation, physical sickness, and injury all cause grief. Yes, even retirement can bring grief.

Edgar Jackson described grief in this way: "Grief is a young widow who must seek a means to bring up her three children, alone. Grief is the angry reaction of a man so filled with shocked uncertainty and confusion that he strikes out at the nearest person. Grief is a mother walking daily to a nearby cemetery to stand quietly and alone for a few moments before she goes on about the tasks of the day; she knows that part of her is in the cemetery, just as part of her is in her daily work. Grief is the silent, knife-like terror and sadness that comes a hundred times a day, when you start to speak to someone who is no longer there. Grief is the emptiness that comes when you eat alone after eating with another for many years. Grief is teaching yourself somehow to go to bed without saying good night to the one who has died. Grief is the helpless wishing that things were different when you know they are not and never will be again. Grief is a whole cluster of adjustments, apprehensions, and uncertainties that strike life in its forward progress and make it difficult to . . . redirect the energies of life."[4] That's grief.

There can be good in our grief when we realize that the "stages of grieving" often blend and merge together. Psalm 91:2 says, "I will say of the Lord, 'He is my refuge and my

4. Jackson, *For the Living,* 21.

fortress, my God, in whom I trust.'" We may understand academically that the stages we go through in the grieving process are shock, denial, resentment, anger, acceptance, and readjustment. But often these stages all seem to blend together. Sometimes we simply must just trust the God of all comfort. Sometimes we must just accept the fact that God IS our refuge and fortress. It's easy to understand the stages academically, in our heads, but to trust God—that is another matter. We can think through these reactions. But to experientially move through these stages is a whole different issue. And what makes it more difficult is that the phases and stages are not clear-cut. The stages of grief differ from person to person. The goal is to accept the fact that God is our refuge and our fortress.

There can be good in our grief when we remember that God is always with us and covers us. Psalm 91:3–8 says, "Surely he will save you from the fowler's snare and from the deadly pestilence. He will cover you with his feathers, and under his wings you will find refuge; his faithfulness will be your shield and rampart. You will not fear the terror of night, nor the arrow that flies by day, nor the pestilence that stalks in the darkness, nor the plague that destroys at mid-day. A thousand may fall at your side, ten thousand at your right hand, but it will not come near you. You will only ob-serve with your eyes and see the punishment of the wicked." Have you ever watched a mother protect her child? Have you ever seen cats, chickens, or birds with their little ones? The mother bird covers her tiny baby birds with her wings. They find refuge in the mother's faithfulness. "He will cover you with his feathers, and under his wings you will find refuge; his faithfulness will be your shield and rampart" (v. 4).

There can be good in our grief when we let it open a door of opportunity to help someone else. Psalm 91:9–12 says, "If you make the Most High your dwelling—even the Lord, who is my refuge—then no harm will befall you, no disaster will come near your tent. For he will command his angels concerning you to guard you in all your ways; they will lift you up in their hands, so that you will not strike your foot against a stone." Hebrews 13:5b says, "Never will I leave you; never will I forsake you." Moving through the grieving process actually gives us an opportunity to grow and to share God's comfort and love with others. God has promised to lift us up; he has promised to be with us always, and that is something we need to share with others going through challenging times. Grief is often associated with a loss because of death. But grief can be the loss of a relationship. No matter what the challenge we can use that as an opportunity to strengthen others.

There can be good in our grief when it helps us readjust our priorities and focus on God, his love, and his Word. Psalm 91:13–16 says, "You will tread upon the lion and the cobra; you will trample the great lion and the serpent. 'Because he loves me,' says the Lord, 'I will rescue him; I will protect him, for he acknowledges my name. He will call upon me, and I will answer him; I will be with him in trouble, I will deliver him and honor him. With long life will I satisfy him and show him my salvation.'" Grief can help us readjust our priorities. Grief has a way of helping us acknowledge his name. Grief draws us back to our Lord, his love, and his Word. Looking back on my own life, each time I have experienced grief, there have been great lessons to be learned. God never promised an easy journey, but God did promise to be with us through it all. By the grace of God, we grow through our trials; we gain strength. We become stronger persons as a result. Grief helps us readjust our priorities and focus on God and God alone.

Four Misunderstandings about Grief

Perhaps nothing we do in life is more important than helping people we love during times of grief. Conversely, we need family and friends during our times of grief. Understanding the misunderstandings and myths of grief will help us both comfort others and receive comfort.

1. The myth that remembering a loved one will increase grief.
2. The myth that grief is an enemy to be avoided.
3. The myth that denial of grief will make it go away.
4. The myth that sympathy will make grief worse.

Perhaps the first misunderstanding about grieving is related to memory. Most of us think it hurts too much to remember a painful experience. In so thinking, we try to cover up the reality of the loss. Years ago, when I conducted a funeral, I used words that would lessen the impact of the reality that the loved one had "died." I am not suggesting that we be insensitive; quite the contrary. I am suggesting that we be extremely sensitive, but not misleading. The reality is that someone is dying or has died. We come for comfort. We come to reflect upon that person's life. We come not to forget, but to remember. "Grief is not a process of forgetting, it is a process of learning to cope while we remember."[5]

Sometimes we must let go with our hands and hold on to precious memories with our heart. It's important that we keep those two factors in proper perspective: what to let go of and what to hold on to. Memory becomes an important part of that process. We need to let go of the physical being. But equally important, we will need to hold on to the

5. Manning, *Gift of Significance*, 31.

wonderful memories with our heart. Letting go and holding on are very important parts of the grieving process.

The second misunderstanding about grief is that grief is an enemy. Grief is actually a friend that brings healing. Grief is a positive force for healing. Grief is *not* something to be feared and avoided.

Some years ago I conducted a funeral for an elderly woman and could not help but notice a young grandson who was in perfect emotional control throughout the entire service. He seemed to show no emotion whatsoever. I was interested in how or why he would be seemingly so emotionally detached. However, when the service concluded at the graveside, he slowly and quietly walked away quite a distance. While everyone was quietly reflecting on the life that had been memorialized, I kept a steady eye on the young man. He walked further and further away until at one point, he dropped to his knees. I watched him reach his hands to the sky, and I heard a yell of release that turned into wailing. He was finally beginning to grieve. A major misunderstanding we sometimes face is that grief is our enemy to be avoided. In reality, grief is a dear friend.

A third misunderstanding we sometimes have is that if we do not talk about grief—if we deny it—it will go away. Actually the opposite is true. "Grief that is left to fester often exemplifies itself in some of the things we call social problems."[6] People go through grief in different ways and on different timelines. Women will often enter grief immediately while men will hold back and deny and avoid their feelings. Sometimes these simple differences can drive a wedge between friends or even family members. As we minister to senior adults and help them deal with losses in life, we must

6. Ibid., 32.

help them face reality. We must sensitively and lovingly listen and guide grieving people toward a loving relationship with our Lord.

A fourth misunderstanding is that sometimes sympathy makes it worse. I could hardly believe my ears at a ministerial breakfast one morning. One of the members from another church in the community had visited our morning worship service. We have an excellent follow-up ministry, so I became aware of this elderly man immediately. Learning that he had recently lost his wife but that he was an active member of another church, I hesitated to make a home visit. Instead, I decided to contact the senior pastor of his church. After a week went by, I wondered if the elderly man would be back in our worship service. You guessed it, the next week he was back in worship. At this point, I felt compelled to talk with the elderly man's pastor. When I met with the pastor at a ministerial breakfast and shared with him that one of his members was in worship two Sundays, I was shocked at his response. To my amazement, the pastor used a phrase that surprised me: "crybaby." Indeed the man was extremely emotional, but for good reason. The man was in desperate need of love, caring, and sympathy. He needed help in the grieving process. In many cases, we misunderstand the healing process in thinking that people should get over it.

I have found it helpful to encourage people to understand that loss, and death in particular, is better understood as a transition. When we realize that life is limited, we can get on with *living* to a maximum. The apostle Paul wrote about death for the believer as a transition. In 1 Thessalonians 4:13–18 he wrote, "Brothers and sisters, we do not want you to be ignorant about those who fall asleep, or to grieve like the rest of men, who have no hope. We believe that Jesus died and rose again and so we believe that God will bring with

Jesus those who have fallen asleep in him. According to the Lord's own word, we tell you that we who are still alive, who are left till the coming of the Lord, will certainly not precede those who have fallen asleep. For the Lord himself will come down from Heaven, with a loud command, with the voice of the archangel and with the trumpet call of God, and the dead in Christ will rise first. After that, we who are still alive and are left will be caught up together with them in the clouds to meet the Lord in the air. And so we will be with the Lord forever. Therefore encourage each other with these words." For the Christian, and for the non-Christian, dying is a transition. We are moving from the physical to the spiritual.

Dying involves saying goodbye to a loved one. It's a time of letting go. It's a time of remembering. Dying "rituals" allow people time to face the transition that is before them. These rituals give people dignity and preparation.

I've mentioned *The Gift of Significance*, written by Doug Manning already. Manning carefully outlines these important steps of transition. Manning tells us there is no need to whisper things as our loved one comes closer to the transition of leaving this physical earth; that person is very aware of that fact. The issue is not *whether* they should know. The issue is *can we face it with them?*[7] Tossing scriptures at sick people does not help. Even "saying a prayer" often leaves an emptiness. True caring on a feeling level is most helpful.

When my father was dying I was in a church in northern California. My parents were in Southern California, living in retirement. I had received news that my dad was very ill. We had visited my parents numerous times. I knew the family doctor. I felt comfortable that when the critical time arrived, I would have time to spend closing hours with

7. Ibid., 13.

my dad. However, one day when I called the hospital to talk with my dad, the nurse told me that he was in a coma. I insisted that she place the telephone receiver next to his ear. She reminded me that he had not responded to anyone or anything for a day or two. When she placed the telephone receiver next to his ear and I said, "Dad, how are you?" I heard these words: "David, is that *you*?" Those were the last words he spoke.

We must pray, yes, but we must learn to be sensitive to the Spirit's leading. We must allow people time to deal with their feelings. We must allow those who are grieving to talk about their feelings. Hospice is a wonderful ministry because it allows people to move through the transition of dying with dignity. I have learned something about clergy: Too often clergy are more interested in conversation and conversion than they are in comfort. Perhaps this is because we have such strong biblical and theological convictions. We have the answers. We offer hope to the hopeless. We have a message to present to those in need. But often we present that message inappropriately or at the wrong time. It hurts so much to talk and to remember, but it hurts much more to remember and *not* talk.

Some Reminders

So often we think a grieving person needs or wants conversation when in reality all that is wanted and needed is quiet comfort.

Grief is not an enemy.

People need permission to grieve.

Grief takes time. It is *not* wallowing; it usually lasts two years.

It has been said that "Grief is like peeling an onion; it comes off one layer at a time, and you cry a lot."[8]

Divorce, death, miscarriage, suicide, broken relationships and friendships, moving to a new city, a job change: all of these transitions take time for healing. The well-known steps of recovery—shock, anger, resentment, and readjustment—become extremely important in helping people through loss.

The reconstruction process is time-consuming, and we need a lot of patience during this process. We're helping people move on. We're helping them reestablish their lives. We're taking broken lives and fostering healing.

This means that we too must learn to cope in a new way. We must help those who are grieving to cope in new ways. We must help people understand that it's important that they remember. In our senior adult ministry, we are not trying to help people forget loved ones. We're trying to help them live with the loved ones not being here. There is a big difference. In all of this we must know when to be available and when to hug. We must know when to talk and when to be silent. We must know when people are feeling happy and when they're feeling sad. For this reason, we have begun a specific ministry at our church called "Care Ministry." The Care Ministry not only sends flowers and cards but also provides food and friendship. More importantly, this ministry continues on when the family goes back home and the house is empty. The real ministry of caring begins when everyone has left and the house is quiet.

8. Ibid., 38.

Doug Manning says, "Grief only comes in one size—extra-large." He goes on to point out that there are two important events in grief and pain:

- When the pain starts.
- When the person decides to do something about the pain.[9]

George Marshall came up with a three-step formula for dealing with conflict due to grief: Let the other person tell their story. Let the other person tell their *whole* story. Let the other person tell their whole story *first*. In grief, listen; let the person tell their story. "After all of the books have been read, the seminars experienced, and the speeches heard, someone must reach out and touch."[10]

COMMUNICATION AND CARING

"Several years ago a government-sponsored study discovered that when people had personal problems, only 28 percent of them went to professional counselors or clinics. Approximately 29 percent consulted their family physician and 42 percent sought help from clergymen. Little wonder that doctors are overworked and pastors are swamped with impossible caseloads—so much so that thousands of needy people are doing what they have done for centuries—turning to friends for advice and encouragement in times of need."[11]

Caring for and helping others is mentioned many times in the Bible. Consider, for example, some of the ways in which God helps people. Look up the following passages, and note the ways in which God helps: Psalm 46:1,

9. Ibid., 44.
10. Ibid., 48.
11. Collins, *How to Be a People Helper,* 33–35.

Hebrews 4:16, Hebrews 13:6, Proverbs 3:5–6, Isaiah 40:31, and Philippians 4:19.

God often uses us to help others. The Bible even commands that we be dedicated people helpers. For example, look up the following verses, and jot down what we are expected to do when people around us are in need: Matthew 10:8, Romans 12:15 and 12:20, Galatians 6:2, and 1 John 3:17.

According to the Bible, it's imperative that Christians reach out to and love others. A first step to being an effective caring and loving person is to invite Christ into our lives to live there and control us: "Dear friends, let us love one another, for love comes from God. Everyone who loves has been born of God and knows God. Whoever does not love does not know God, because God is love" (1 John 4:7–8).

7

Claim God's Promises

Have I not commanded you? Be strong and coura-
geous. Do not be terrified; do not be discouraged, for
the LORD your God will be with you wherever you go.
(Josh 1:9)

GOD IS FAITHFUL

MANY PEOPLE do not experience successful aging simply because they do not claim God's blessings. God
does have a wonderful plan for us. We sometimes go astray
because we don't apply biblical principles to daily living. The
goal of this chapter is to encourage you to claim God's blessing of peace.

Psalm 73 is about claiming God's promises when things
are down. This psalm gives practical help to people who are
discouraged, depressed, and facing loss and grief.[1] There are
seven practical suggestions within the psalm for claiming
God's promises. First, we must *realize* that we simply don't
understand. Psalm 73:16 says, "When I tried to understand
all this, it was oppressive to me." Sometimes we simply don't

1. Ray Stedman, *Folk Psalms of Faith,* 201–18, offers encouragement for
applying this psalm.

understand why we're going through a situation. Our response must be as the opening verse of this psalm: "Surely God is good to Israel, to those who are pure in heart."

Second, we must *reflect*, pause and look up into the presence of God. Psalm 73:17 says, "Till I entered the sanctuary of God; then I understood their final destiny." Sometimes we must look into the presence of a God who is all-powerful and simply realize that God knows and we do not. When we come into the presence of God, we can relax in God's hands. He is in control when we are not. Sometimes God uses these experiences of allowing us to be down so that we will look up.

Third, we must *reevaluate* our thinking. Psalm 73:21–22 says, "When my heart was grieved and my spirit embittered, I was senseless and ignorant . . . Yet . . . You hold me by my right hand." Bitterness is a reality of life when grief overtakes us. Pain and suffering do strange things to people. We begin to question God. It's easy to become angry. It's easy to begin asking "why" questions. Let God answer your questions.

I read about a little girl who was dying of leukemia. She asked the nurse for a crying doll. When the nurse asked why, she replied, "Mommy and I need to cry. Mommy won't cry in front of me, and I can't cry if Mommy doesn't. If we had a crying doll, all three of us could cry together. I think we'd feel better."

Fourth, we must *recognize* that we do not see the big picture. Psalm 73:23–24 says, "Yet I am always with you; you hold me by my right hand. You guide me with your counsel, and afterward you will take me into glory." God sees the big picture. We must not lose perspective. As Martin Luther said, "Without trials . . . a person can neither know Scripture or faith, nor can he fear and love God. If he has never suffered, he cannot understand what hope is."[2] We must look up, be quiet, and realize that we simply do not understand. Look up into the presence of God. Look up to see the big picture and not lose perspective.

Fifth, we must *remember* that God still loves us. Psalm 73:23–24 says, "Yet I am always with you; you hold me by my right hand. You guide me with your counsel, and afterward you will take me into glory." God will guide you with counsel. Then we can say afterward, "*You* will take me to glory!" (emphasis mine).

A pastor friend had just received news of a terminal illness. That next Sunday he told his congregation the news. He had walked five miles from the doctor's office to his home. He had sat looking at the mountains. He had looked at giant trees and the river and the big blue sky. He had said out loud, "I may not see you long, but I'll be alive. River, I'll be alive after you are dry. Trees, I will be alive when you have fallen. Hope lies beyond the grave!" Death is not the end. Innumerable, indescribable, eternal glories are ahead for those who know the Lord!

I'm an avid Arizona Diamondbacks fan. One of my favorite expressions is "the ballgame's not over yet." The psalmist reminds us that we will not perish. We must join with the psalmist in saying, "It is good to be near God. I have made the Sovereign Lord my refuge" (Ps 73:28). God is faithful. Look up and remember that God is still on the throne. God *is* indeed in full control.

One of the biggest challenges you might ever face in your marriage is finding your way after losing your spouse. No words can explain the emptiness. Certainly your spouse

2. "Surprised by Suffering," http://www.lcms.org/page.aspx?pid=868.

would want you to become what some call a "creative survivor"—seeking ways to go on in spite of your loss and grief. The truth is that you must press on, and with God's help, you will survive. Life will never be the same, but you must move ahead. While the pain you feel is excruciating, these keys can help you move ahead when you're ready:

- Take one step at a time. You have this moment in time—right now. You can't do much about yesterday and you have no guarantees for tomorrow. You have today. Take a small step forward each day. It might help to write out your steps by keeping a journal of your feelings, getting involved in a grief group, or taking that first step of going to church the first time after the loss of your spouse. If you've been involved in a church together, going back after your spouse's death is a huge step. It's a bit easier if you go with someone and don't sit alone.

- Don't make quick decisions. Most counselors encourage people to not make any big decisions for at least a year, and that's good advice. You might feel inclined to sell your house or move across the country. But whatever decision you make, time will greatly help you make it wisely. Feelings change and you may make decisions that you regret later.

- Remember that healing takes time.[3] Just as a physical injury takes time to mend, emotional and spiritual anguish require time, patience, and faith to heal. Perspective is often lost during painful times, and scripture passages may give a fresh reminder of God's love and faithfulness.

3. You might find my book with that title, *Healing Takes Time*, to be a helpful resource.

- Take steps to relieve loneliness. Loneliness can be crippling. It will take real effort to begin to get back on the road of socialization. Don't drop out of church or social groups you and your spouse enjoyed. In fact, if you've stayed away because your spouse battled a long illness, think of this as a time to reconnect.

- Let others help. It is amazing how God can use people to help you rebuild your life. In addition to family members, look to grief support groups, activities of interest, fellowship groups, care groups, and other ministries in your church and community to provide help you need.

- Find ways to ease the adjustment. You need to do a lot of talking, so resist your urge to withdraw. Again, reconnect with family members and friends. Ask your pastor if you can meet for coffee. Don't be afraid to seek professional counseling help if you feel like you're not getting over your grief in the ways you expected. As you tell your stories of pain, your grief will begin to lessen over time.

- Try not to dwell on regrets. After the loss of your spouse, you'll naturally think about the past. Even if you faced conflicts or spoke hurtful words during your marriage, focus on the many happy times in your marriage.

PREPARING FOR A NEW VIEW OF MARRIAGE

While attending a marriage seminar on communication, Tom, age seventy-two, and his wife Peg, age seventy, listened to the instructor declare, "It is essential that husbands and wives know the things that are important to each other." He looked at Tom and asked, "Can you describe your wife's favorite flower?" Tom leaned over, touched his wife's arm gently and whispered, "Pillsbury All-Purpose, isn't it?" The rest of the story is not pleasant.

Marriage has cycles. Most couples begin their marriage with high expectations. Marriage vows, easily spoken when you're at the altar, can be challenging to live out over the test of thirty, forty, fifty, sixty, or seventy years. When things get rough, it takes hard work to invest in your marriage. Don't be afraid to seek counsel from your pastor or a professional marriage counselor. Some issues you might be facing include:

- The need for affection and sexual intimacy.
- The need for companionship.
- The need for family when you find yourself alone.
- The need for financial security as you grow older together.
- The need for spiritual intimacy together with God.

How can you rediscover the fulfillment you'd hoped for in marriage? The bottom line is commitment—focusing on the covenant you and your spouse made to each other before God.

You might want to go out to your favorite breakfast spot or just sit on your patio or deck and talk about how you can make the following commitments together. Probe a bit beyond the surface—instead of just words, decide what actions you can take to live out each commitment in your marriage.

Drawing Near to God as a Couple

There are many issues couples face that have the potential for bringing them closer together and as a couple, closer to God. However, if not handled appropriate, these same issues can build walls between them and weaken their relationship with God. Find a quiet place to discuss each of the following issues together.

- Disappointments: Our disappointments can be steps of growth as we face them together honestly and give them to God.

- Relationship with each other: Our relationship with each other must be based on our relationship with God. He is the giver of life and is able to keep our marriage alive, which will give us a new view of our marriage.

- Dependence on God: Our dependence on God strengthens our interdependence with each other.

- Absolute faithfulness: Our commitment will be strengthened as we recommit ourselves to absolute faithfulness to one another and to God.

My wife and I were walking hand in hand along the street near a university not long ago. Here we were, two older folks strolling along like two kids in love. A small group of college students came toward us and one college student said very audibly, "Awe, that's so sweet!" Just the way she said it made it clear that we had made a positive impression on her.

After forty-three years of marriage my wife and I have learned that a strong marriage involves commitment through not only the good times when it is easy and life seems so good, but through the challenging times when we grow and learn great lessons of life.

Preparing for Potential Remarriage

It has well been said that following the loss of a spouse, the surviving spouse needs to wait at least one full year before making big changes in life. As the grieving and healing takes place often new relationships begin to form. With older adults there are some unique challenges. Many older adults today are asking clergy to perform a "lawful covenant" marriage rather than a "legal contract" marriage because their spouse is deceased and there are financial implications.

For example, John, age seventy-one, is receiving Social Security benefits of one thousand dollars a month, and his wife, Nancy, age eighty-six, is receiving six hundred dollars a month in benefits. If John dies, Nancy receives the higher of the two amounts, one thousand dollars monthly. However, if Nancy remarries, the situation changes and she'll only receive her original benefit of six hundred dollars. For this reason many adults are choosing not to get legally married. Sometimes they choose to live together unmarried, and sometimes they ask clergy to perform a service of commitment that isn't legally recorded by the state. There may be other legal and financial reasons as well that prevent older adults from wanting to remarry legally.

So is marriage a "contract" or a mutually binding agreement between a man and a woman recognized as a legal civil contract by the state, which issues licenses for people to enter into such contracts? Or is marriage a "covenant" between a man and a woman pledging themselves before God, their Creator, to become "one flesh" as long as they live? In the United States, the first is the primary concept. The fact is that religious (church) ceremonies are accepted on a legal basis. Confusion arises because clergy are permitted to act as "agents for the state" to perform legal (contract) marriage ceremonies within the religious (covenant) marriage setting.

Moral and Ethical Issues of 'Secret' Marriage

There are four reasons why I would not perform a marriage kept secret from the state.

1. Marriage is a legal contract that's sanctioned by the state. Marriage is established by God (Gen 2–3; Matt 19:5; Mark 10:7–8; Eph 5:22–23). Financial pressures may seem to force people to live together, but at the same time, these are the same arguments that some young people give. They want to have physical pleasures of marriage, but they don't formalize the relationship because they'd lose financial rewards (alimony, welfare benefits, and so on). At some point people need to ask whether they're willing to do what is right in God's sight even if there are financial penalties for doing so. The supernatural aspect must be factored into the equation. When we choose to live a godly life and are willing to sacrifice for it, God honors this choice. He may bless us financially for the financial sacrifice we have made. He may bless us by showing us how to enjoy the simpler things in life. He may bless us in ways having nothing to do with finances: by bringing people into our lives that bring us joy, by softening our heart and allowing us to forgive those who have wronged us, by giving us peace where there once was turmoil. Because the law says that we need a license, I believe that as Christians we should obey.

2. Ceremonies kept secret from the state offer a bad example. This bad example impacts the children, grandchildren, other family members, and the rest of the congregation. We need to continue to uphold the biblical standards that marriage is God's ideal and urge couples to make the tough choice between economics and

upholding biblical views. These couples could continue to be friends in celibacy and live as single people. Are sex and economics more important to most people than moral values? Somehow, society, including Christian couples, has caved in to economic excuses for living together without legal license.

3. Marriage has a biblical fabric. The fabric of marriage is a spiritual and legal commitment, and as a witness to strengthen family life, supersedes any economic factor. Jesus said that we should render to Caesar what is Caesar's and to God what is God's. Mark 10 refers to a deep commitment to a full marriage covenant. A legal marriage in the United States requires a license. Romans 13:1 tells us that we have a responsibility to deal with the governing authorities and that we're to live according to the laws of our country. Not legalizing marriage means trying to use the ends to justify the means, and this goes completely against Christian ethics. If we discourage young couples from living together for financial reasons, we should hold older adults to the same standard. I wonder if the usual concern of "cannot remarry for financial reasons" really means "find it financially less robust to remarry." These are wisdom issues in which prior decisions may be coming home to roost. Isn't the issue often a matter of diminished standard of living rather impoverishment or impossibility?

4. Intentional deception is incompatible with the biblical model. An intentional nondisclosure of the marriage to the church, the public, or the governing authorities indicates an unwillingness to adhere to the biblical model of marriage. This is especially true in cases where individuals seek to gain the financial or social

advantages of being single, while still wanting to enjoy the benefits of marriage. Marriage is for better or for worse; it's not a halfway commitment. It seems to me the issue is honesty. I wouldn't be able to encourage a couple to continue to receive governmental revenues based on what amounts to deception, and I could not bring in the church, which I represent by performing such a ceremony, as a partner in the deception.[4]

4. Gallagher, "Marriage Matters," 22–23.

8

Keep Your Spirits High

A person's steps are directed by the LORD. How then can anyone understand his own way? (Prov 20:24)

Consider it pure joy, my brothers and sisters, whenever you face trials of many kinds, because you know that the testing of your faith develops perseverance. Perseverance must finish its work so that you may be mature and complete, not lacking anything. If any of you lacks wisdom, he should ask God, who gives generously to all without finding fault, and it will be given to him. But when he asks, he must believe and not doubt, because he who doubts is like a wave of the sea, blown and tossed by the wind. (Jas 1:2–6)

PREPARING FOR OUR ELDERLY YEARS

MANY RESOURCES are available to help us age in a healthy way. We may not be aware of the physical, financial, emotional, spiritual, or material resources available today. Sometimes we fail to notice God's abundant plan for successful aging because we have not made the most of the resources available to us, thereby missing both the human and divine help.

In this chapter, I would like to offer you some practical advice by explaining and simplifying vocabulary used by physicians, nurses, social workers and care centers. People who are aging or have parents or friends who are aging need help knowing what resources are available. My goal in this chapter is to help cut through the mountains of governmental bureaucracy and help people make wise, intelligent, and even godly decisions.

Many people have found that having all necessary information and documents for later years of life is very helpful. One way to do this is to prepare a notebook that contains these important legal documents:

- A Last Will and Testament

- Revocable Living Trust

- General Power of Attorney

- Specific Power of Attorney

- Letters of Notification of Death

It is amazing how complex our society has become in recent years, and so a simple notebook with copies of documents can be invaluable. Your church may also want to maintain a card file giving basic emergency contact information on how to reach family members. There are sample emergency forms included in this chapter.

Along with the joys of aging come health issues that sometimes present special challenges. The aging process might raise a variety of psychological, social, spiritual, and physical health concerns for Boomers and Builders. For example, their concerns might include dealing with chronic illness or disability, the loss of friends and family members, and their own impending mortality. They might also feel that they do not have the resources, coping skills, or social support to shape their life according to their needs and desires.

Up to this point, we've focused on active adults. However, there are seniors who are homebound or in need of either short- or long-term care. It's important that these characteristics be considered as well. Long life spans and changing living patterns have made the later senior years a new and somewhat uncharted adventure.

Preparing for Changing Lifestyles

Most couples in later-in-life marriages face decisions about where to live. Maybe you've owned your home for years, or maybe you decided to buy a motor home and you spend your days traveling across the country. Chances are you've been around long enough to know that no living situation is permanent.

As you and your spouse face the possibility of changing your living situation—whether now or many years down the road, it helps to know the language. Here's a brief list of some key vocabulary words:

- Independent living. Requires little or no assistance with the activities of daily living.

- Telephone reassurance. Provides a daily call for those who live alone, who are anxious about safety or security, or who face health challenges.

- Transportation services. Offers rides to elderly or disabled persons who don't have private transportation or who can't use public transportation.

- Home delivered meal services. Services that bring healthy meals right to the home of the homebound.

- Home support. Provides assistance within the home

by external agencies or persons who manage daily living tasks such as housekeeping, laundry, limited maintenance, meals, bathing, and so forth.

- Self-care. The senior self-manages the simple and complex activities of daily living including a limited amount of medical care.

- Assisted living. Similar to home support services, but generally provided within an apartment or cottage in a retirement center setting.

- Continuing care retirement or lifecare. A retirement center that provides shelter, care, and services (including nursing services) for as long as the resident lives in the facility in return for a one-time entrance charge and monthly fees.

- Counseling services. Individuals or agencies that provide families guidance and support in solving problems and making decisions.

- Friendly visiting services. Provides regularly scheduled visits for the homebound or isolated; provides companionship and expresses concern for the individual's well-being.

- Adult day care. Provides planned, supervised activities and meals in a group setting for adults during all or part of a day.

- Health care center. Offers three levels of nursing care: personal care, skilled care, and sub-acute care.[1]

- Personal care. The lowest level of care provided within a skilled nursing care center. This lowest

---

1. Specific terms and licensing requirements vary from state to state. For an extensive listing of State Agencies on Aging, see Houston and Parker, *Vision for the Aging Church*, 266–72.

level of care is available to those who have control of their bladder and bowels, but who must be given medications by a licensed member of the nursing staff.

- Skilled care. The medium level of care offered between personal care and skilled nursing care. Also called Intermediate care.

- Sub-acute care. The highest level of medical care given in a skilled nursing setting.

- Adult foster care. Enables persons to live with families or individuals who are willing to share their homes. These arrangements vary greatly from state to state, but can include sharing responsibilities such as housekeeping and meal preparation, or may include these types of services as part of the contracted fee. Check with state and county agencies to see the services these facilities are licensed to provide in your state.

- Alzheimer's care. Provides care to persons with Alzheimer's, usually in a hospital or skilled nursing facility setting.

- Group home. Refers to a residential house converted to accommodate several senior adults in a home setting and atmosphere. Check with state and county agencies to see the services these facilities are licensed to provide in your area.

- Hospice care. Medical and support services for individuals diagnosed with a terminal illness and who have a short life expectancy.

- Occupational therapy. Medical services that promote rehabilitation of social, recreational, and body mechanics needed to perform the activities of daily life.

- Physical therapy. Medical services that promote rehabilitation of the body through exercise and other types of stimulation.

- Residential care. Provided in a retirement center setting with twenty-four-hour supervision. Also called supervisory care.

- Respite care. Provides residential care, usually for less than a month. This break from the ongoing caregiving responsibilities relieves caregivers and allows them to refresh, renew, and revitalize themselves.

- Speech therapy. Medical services promoting rehabilitation of speech.

- Supervisory care. Another term for residential care.[2]

Advances in health care have made living with disabilities and caregiving in the later years of life both a reality and a challenging responsibility. There are many options of care available today in all parts of the country. As we age it is important that we become familiar with the options available.

Identifying Needs and Services

Identifying your needs and the services to meet those needs is the first step in making the right choice for your future, or the future of a loved one. Begin by looking at the extent of the health issues or disabilities and evaluate whether they interfere with independence. Are you really able to care for yourself? Is another individual able to care for him or herself? Use the following checklist of daily living activities

2. Jakes, *Decision is Yours*, 21–24.

to help determine if you or another person is independent, needs help to perform a task, or is unable to do so at all:

Daily Activities Independence Checklist

	Yes	No
Walking: Can the individual move about without devices or help from another person?		
Transferring: Can he change positions from bed to chair to toilet without assistance?		
Toileting: Can he get to the bathroom and use all of the facilities?		
Bathing: Can she get to the bathroom, prepare hot water, get into the tub or shower, and wash unassisted?		
Dressing and Grooming: Can the individual dress without assistance, put on artificial limbs or braces, and perform grooming tasks such as washing hair or shaving?		
Eating: Can he feed himself?		
Food Preparation: Can she prepare or heat meals?		
Housekeeping: Can the individual do minimal cleaning in the house and do the laundry?		
Shopping: Can she plan and prepare meals and also do the necessary grocery shopping?		
Medicine: Can she reliably take the correct medication at the proper time?		
Telephone: Can he use the telephone to communicate with others or to request help?		
Communication of Needs: Can the individual make needs and desires known by any means of communication?		
Security: Can the individual exercise care in locking windows and doors?		
Safety: Can she recognize and correct hazardous conditions in the home?		
Orientation: Is he accurately aware of places, people, days, and years?		

Decision Making: Can the individual make appropriate choices?		
Medical Needs: Are there conditions that would require skilled nursing care?		
Nighttime Care: Can the individual be left alone at night and can he call for help if needed?		

Scoring: If you answered no to 15 questions or more, this may be an indication of the need for twenty-four-hour care such as skilled care, supervisory care, or assisted living care. If you answered no on 7 or more questions, this may indicate the need for in-home or out-of-home supportive services such as adult day health care, respite service or home companions, in-home homemakers, or health aides.[3]

If you want help in evaluating the patient and family needs, a variety of resources are available to provide this service. When being discharged from a hospital, discharge plans should be discussed with the social services department of the hospital. They can make recommendations and will assist in the implementation of the care needed. A case manager can evaluate needs and arrange for the provision of needed services. Nurses employed by home health agencies may assist the individual and/or caregiver in evaluating and arranging for needed help.

Once strengths and problems are identified, you can begin to match needs with available long- and short-term care services. If the activities of daily living can be managed independently, the choice may be to remain in the present home with the help of support services.

If you discover that more specialized services are needed, the decision might be to remain in the present home and

3. This chart and its scoring are from *How Do I Find It?*, 4–11.

make use of home health care services. These might include nursing care, home health aides, and therapists.

Even with these kinds of help, remaining at home may not be possible. If some protection, supervision, or help with daily activities is needed, the best solution might be to change residence to a supervisory care home where room, board, and supervision are provided. Such homes require a resident to be able to care for themselves and to get around without help. If more assistance and twenty-four-hour supervision is recommended, it may be desirable to consider residence in an adult care home.

If health problems or disabilities require round-the-clock nursing care, the best decision might be to change residence to a health care center (nursing home) where twenty-four-hour nursing and rehabilitation services are provided.

Socialization in a supervised setting can make a long illness less trying for a family. Adult day care provides professionally supervised recreation and socialization, as well as nutrition and health supervision. In assisting families, adult day care can help prevent premature or inappropriate institutionalization. Respite is provided for caregivers allowing them to pursue necessary shopping and errand activities while their family member enjoys a safe and stimulating environment.

Hospice services are available both in-home and in dedicated facilities during a final illness. Because of the pioneering work of Cicely Saunders, a compassionate physician in England, the last months of life need not be spent in isolation, pain, and fear. Sensitive volunteers and professionals can provide care and support through hospice services licensed by the state. When services are given by a Medicare approved hospice, the costs are covered 100 percent through the Medicare hospice benefit.

It is helpful to know the distinction between various types of long- and short-term care. Home health agencies which are state licensed and are Medicare certified provide periodic nursing care, as needed, and at least one other service in the home. Care is given only under a physician's direction. A specific plan of treatment is written for each person. Qualified nurses and therapists provide or supervise the care. In addition to nursing care, home health agencies provide one or more of the following services:

Physical Therapy: Supervised exercises, treatment, training, and education to renew or increase physical abilities.

Occupational Therapy: Supervised exercises and other activities to renew or increase the ability to perform daily living tasks such as dressing, eating, homemaking, and leisure activities.

Speech Therapy: Supervised activities to renew or increase speech and language abilities.

Medical Social Service: Counseling individuals and their families to help them in adjusting to physical and emotional problems.[4]

Nutritional Counseling: Information on nutritional care, special diets, meal times, and food management.

ELDER LAW

Elder law is a relatively new area of legal practice that focuses on the legal needs of older adults, incapacitated people, and their families. Some of these issues in the legal realm include long-term care planning, planning around public benefits such as Medicare and Medicaid, estate planning, advance planning for incapacity, elder abuse, elder financial exploitation, and guardianship and conservatorship court

4. Jakes, *Decision is Yours*, 21–24. Jakes contributed ideas on the categories of physical, occupational, and speech therapy.

proceedings. All of these are important as singles and couples reach their later years.

Perhaps long-term care planning tops this list. Long-term care planning involves determining if you can afford to pay for future care in a skilled nursing care center or assisted living center. If you don't have sufficient income and savings to pay for this care, you need to seek legal and financial planning assistance so you can preserve your assets while also qualifying for Medicare and Medicaid.

A central part of elder law involves estate planning. Estate planning includes written documents that express how you want your assets to be owned, managed, and preserved during your lifetime, and how you want assets allocated after you die. Wills and trusts are common ways to distribute your assets after you die. Trusts have the added benefit of avoiding probate.

You might also want to establish legal relationships with individuals who will guard your interests. For example, a financial power of attorney appoints an agent to manage your financial affairs in the event you become incapacitated. A health care power of attorney appoints an agent to make health care decisions for you in the event you become incapacitated.

You can find elder law attorneys by contacting the Area Agency on Aging, National Academy of Elder Law Attorneys, the Alzheimer's Association, or by consulting your local yellow pages.

ELDER FRAUD

There are many types of elder fraud but basically eight key areas of concern:

1. Identification theft. You may not be able to prevent ID theft, but you can minimize your risk by managing your personal information wisely, cautiously, and with heightened sensitivity. Be sure to keep items with personal information in a safe place and limit the cards you carry to what you actually need. Never give out personal information over the telephone, through the mail, or over the Internet unless you have initiated the contact or know who you are dealing with. Deposit outgoing mail in a locked post office collection box or at your local post office. Before you reveal any personally identifying information, find out how it will be used and whether it will be shared with others. Ask to have it kept confidential.

2. Internet scams. Take great caution when purchasing items on the Internet. Get references from family and friends about good online stores and services. Make sure children and grandchildren know how to use the Internet safely. Only use secure servers to process payments. Use your credit card, not your debit card, when you purchase merchandise over the Internet. Your credit card comes equipped with certain protections. Review the privacy policies of any web pages you visit.

3. Fraudulent charities. We all need to be careful to make sure that when we contribute money to a good cause the money is actually used as we intend. Research the organization and ask for annual reports. Review information carefully and make sure you are giving to the charity you think you are giving to. Set a budget for your yearly giving and stick to it. Do not give money to people you do not know and don't give in to high-pressure sales techniques. Check with the Secretary of State web

site of your state to make sure the charity is registered. Look for a more reputable charity to contribute to. You may be amazed to see some of the statistics on charities found at the American Institute of Philanthropy. For any charity you are considering giving money to, check out the percentage spent on charitable causes compared to how much is used for administrative expenses.

4. Home improvement and repair. Use only licensed contractors. Look for a contractor's license number in reputable advertising, such as the telephone book, newspaper service directories, or local online service directories. Or call the Registrar of Contractors for this information. Use companies that provide free estimates and get several estimates for any repair. Compare prices and compare terms. Ask your friends for recommendations or ask the firm for references and of course, check all references. Always get a receipt for any work that you have done. Check the identification of all workers and inspectors and arrange to make payment installments and pay the last installment only after the work is completed to your satisfaction.

5. Telemarketing. Unfortunately, you cannot tell whether a company is legitimate or not by how friendly the caller's voice sounds or by how often the company calls. They believe the longer you stay on the line, they have a better chance of making a sale. Don't be afraid to be rude! Ask the caller to place you on the company's do-not-call list and if they call again, hang up! You may use your answering machine to screen your calls. Never give out bank, credit card, or Social Security information. Do not agree to let someone come pick up a check or other form of payment. If a deal sounds good, ask the

company for more information in writing. A reputable company will be happy to oblige.

6. Sweepstakes. It is illegal for companies to require a purchase to win or to improve the chances of winning in a sweepstakes. If you would like to be removed from "junk mail" offers, write or call the companies directly and ask to be removed from their mailing lists. Always read the fine print before signing anything or sending money. If you don't understand it, think twice before buying. Remember that no purchase is necessary to enter or win a sweepstakes—ever. Do not give out your bank, credit card, or Social Security information—ever.

7. Investments, securities, and insurance. Ask the seller to give you written information about the investment, including financial statements—and read everything very carefully. Get competent help in evaluating your investments from a banker, lawyer, accountant, licensed stockbroker, licensed real estate agent, the Better Business Bureau, or a knowledgeable member of your family. Contact state government agencies for information. Deal with established businesses with solid reputations. Never give out bank account, credit card, or Social Security number information.

8. Home Healthcare: Three types of organizations provide medical care to patients in their own homes: home health agencies, hospice organizations, and private duty (individual or agency). Use great care when looking for private duty medical or personal care services through newspaper or Internet ads. Avoid hiring someone to provide medical or personal care through unlicensed, unregulated agencies unless they conduct thorough background checks or otherwise check the credentials

and references of the people who will be providing the care in your home. State Association for Home Care can provide literature about home care services.[5]

When should you shred information? The easy answer is to shred anything that has a signature, account number, Social Security number, or medical or legal information. Offers of credit should also be shredded since they often include personal information. Even address labels from junk mail and magazines should be shredded! Of course all banking information, including ATM receipts, bank statements, canceled or voided checks, and the like should be shredded.

ELDER ABUSE

"Research indicates that more than *one* in *ten* elders may experience some type of abuse, but only *one* in *five* cases or fewer are reported," according to a March 3, 2010 e-news report by the National Center for Elder Abuse.[6] Older adults may become vulnerable due to isolation, physical or mental disabilities, and dependence on others for assistance. This vulnerability makes them easy targets for physical, emotional, and sexual abuses; neglect; financial exploitation; and fraud. Unfortunately, older victims often do not seek the help they need because they are afraid, ashamed, or reluctant to report the abuser who may be a family member or care provider.

While there has been a lot of media attention about domestic violence in younger couples, the occurrence of

5. This list was compiled by "Beware! Eliminate Exploitation Program (B. E. E. P.), which was funded by the Arizona Attorney General's Office. The program's purpose is to prevent cons, fraud, scams, elder abuse, and identity theft.

6. National Center for Elder Abuse, http://www.ncea.aoa.gov/Main_Site/pdf/publication/NCEA_WhatIsAbuse-2010.pdf, p. 1.

late-life domestic violence is often unrecognized. Older women are among the many victims of spousal abuse, often staying in an abusive marriage for thirty, forty, even fifty years. The victims represent all ethnic, religious, educational, occupational, and socio-economic groups.

It is important for the older person, for friends and family members, and for those working in the caregiving industry to be aware that these incidents do happen. Do not disregard your instincts with regards to elder abuse. If you have been the victim of elder abuse or suspect that someone in your family, or someone under another person's care is being victimized in any of the above ways, do not ignore your suspicions. Report your concerns to authorities so that they can be pursued and, if confirmed, stopped.

Some Things to Remember

It's easy to overreact or become cynical in a complex world. It's important to remember that God is sovereign and we are under his care. To personalize this truth and gain encouragement from it, claim the affirmations below.

I will . . .

- Remember that there are caring people who do want to pray with me and give me guidance, encouragement, and strength.

- Ask for God's guidance, and seek help from friends.

- Let others know of my needs and let them help me.

- Be aware of my surroundings and help myself.

- Remember that God really does want to do a miracle in my life today. I will let God do that miracle.

- *Let go of bitterness and anger, with God's help.*

- Not dwell on any regrets. I will thank God for his

blessings in my life.

- Claim God's grace for my life.
- Thank God for life itself.

9

Relieve Anxiety

Cast all your anxiety on him because he cares for you.
(1 Pet 5:7)

MANY THINGS IN LIFE CAUSE ANXIETY

A Minneapolis couple decided to go to Florida to thaw out during a particularly icy winter. They planned to stay at the same hotel where they spent their honeymoon over thirty years before. Because of their hectic schedules, it was difficult to coordinate their travel schedules. So, the husband left Minneapolis and flew to Florida on Friday and his wife was flying down the following day. The husband checked into the hotel and unlike years ago there was a computer in his room and he decided to send an e-mail to his wife. However, he accidentally left out one letter in her e-mail address and without noticing his error, sent the e-mail to the wrong address.

Meanwhile somewhere in Houston, a widow had just returned home from her husband's funeral. He was a minister who was called home to glory after suffering a heart attack. The widow decided to check her e-mail, expecting messages from relatives and friends. After reading the first message, she screamed and then fainted. The widow's son rushed into the room, found his mother on the floor, and then glanced up and saw the computer screen which read:

> To: My loving wife
> Date: Friday, October 15
> Subject: I have arrived
>
> Dearest Love,
> I know you are surprised to hear from me. They have computers here now and you are allowed to send e-mails to your loved ones. I have just arrived and have been checked in. I see that everything has been prepared for your arrival tomorrow, and look forward to seeing you then. Hope your journey is as eventful as mine was!

You may not have thought of it but non-productiveness may be as stressful as over-productiveness. That is to say that we hear much about overload and burnout but not much about under-load or apathy and boredom. There is an optimal stress level or performance level where we need to be, not overworked and pressured but certainly not bored with nothing to do, leaving us with a feeling of worthlessness. Many different things in life can cause anxiety.

Both ends of the spectrum represent departures from optimal performance, and are precursors of some emotional and physical health issues. Everyone should find his or her optimal stress level for well–balanced stimulation, responsibility, and challenge.

Serious disorders are often preceded by changes in personality or behavior. Excessive stress will elicit these signs while simultaneously eating away at the body's vital systems. When you find yourself thinking, "George had better take it easy or he'll have a heart attack," or "If Tom doesn't stop worrying, he will give himself an ulcer," take your observation seriously.

If you happen to be in the category of having nothing to do, feeling all alone or bored, you need to go back and read through previous sections about volunteerism. Scores of ideas are given on how you may get outside of yourself and help others.

For many however, the opposite is true—we seem to have too many things going on or we have accepted too many responsibilities at our church or service organization where we are serving.

Quiz: Are You Burned Out?

For each statement, circle whether this is rarely true (R) in your life, sometimes true (S), or usually true (U).

R	S	U	
0	1	2	I feel exhausted and run down.
0	1	2	I am irritable.
0	1	2	I get frustrated easily.
0	1	2	I feel helpless.
0	1	2	I have trouble sleeping.
0	1	2	I am discouraged.
0	1	2	I tend to be critical of others.
0	1	2	I tend to be critical of myself.
0	1	2	I want to get away from people.
0	1	2	I would like to change my job, schedule, or routine.
0	1	2	I feel spiritually dull.
0	1	2	I think that my job or daily routine is stressful.
0	1	2	I feel under constant pressure.
0	1	2	I have difficulty being with troubled people.
0	1	2	I am impatient.

| 0 | 1 | 2 | I lack enthusiasm. |

Total Score: _____

If you scored in the range of 16 to 32 points you may be a victim of burnout.[1]

Common Warning Signs

Burnout has many warning signs and may catch you totally off guard. Recovering from burnout requires a commitment to reintroducing balance into your life and lightening a heavy schedule. Some common warning signs include:

- Obsessively working
- Difficulty making decisions
- Excessive daydreaming or fantasizing
- Alcohol in excess
- Antidepressants, tranquillizers
- Disconnected speech or writing
- Constant repetition of the same subject
- Inappropriate anger, hostility, or temper outbursts
- Insomnia, difficulty falling asleep, or frequently awakening
- Missing appointments
- Confusing or forgetting dates, places, times, or other details
- Feeling worthless, inadequate, rejected, insecure
- Difficulty getting along with other people

1. The quiz and scoring were provided by the Bozeman, Montana, Cooperative Extension Service bulletin, "Stress Without Distress," 25.

- Withdrawing from others

Relieving Anxiety

Here are some specific ways to help you relieve anxiety. Try something new and different with any of these suggestions:

- Check out various community activities or classes available through recreation departments, adult education programs, volunteer work opportunities, or community colleges or universities.

- Consider exercise such as walking around your neighborhood or in the woods, bicycling, dancing, playing golf, swimming, gardening, bowling, etc. I heard a cute little story about someone who decided to start exercising. "I feel like my body has gotten totally out of shape, so I got my doctor's permission to join a fitness club and start exercising. I bent, twisted, gyrated, jumped up and down, and perspired for an hour. But by the time I got my leotards on, the class was over."

- For the more physically fit, more strenuous exercise can prove relaxing. These exercises might include jogging, playing tennis, basketball, handball, etc.

- Try some mental exercises to create a sense of peace and tranquility in body and mind. One such exercise involves concentrating on relaxing successive sets of muscles from the tips of your toes to the muscles in your forehead and neck. Other mental relaxation techniques include getting fully involved with a good book, drifting off into a quiet state with music, or focusing on a beautiful scene or drawing, and losing yourself in it.

- Creative activities such as painting, drawing, pottery, carpentry, knitting, and even cooking for fun, can also give you a sense of accomplishment, as well as the peaceful relaxation of concentrating on something you wish to do.

- Whether or not the above suggestions for relaxation work in your case, a sure fire method known down through the ages is the use of a warm bath to take away bodily stress and strain and of course today we have health spas and swimming pools which can add to the relaxation.

Six Simple Strategies to Help Relieve Anxiety

Some years ago my wife and I had the opportunity to see the musical "Annie" when it was playing in Los Angeles at the Pantages Theater. It was an affirmation of life and it was particularly encouraging for me because I was going through a very stressful time. I needed a reminder that tomorrow is another day and it was just time for me to get away from work, anxiety, pressure, and routine.

Here are six simple strategies to help relieve anxiety:

1. Work off stress. Physical exercise is a good way to reduce tension.

2. Talk it out. Sharing concerns and worries with your spouse or good friend will help reduce some of the anxiety you face.

3. Take one thing at a time. Things can get overwhelming if you try to do it all at once. Make a schedule of when you will do certain things so that you have a plan of attack. Put the most urgent duties first.

4. Be flexible. If other people are creating the anxiety in your life, try to see their point of view. Conversely, if you are being "used" by others, learn to be more assertive so that you can better take care of yourself.

5. Think about others. Concentrating too much on yourself will at times contribute to your problem.

6. Try getting your mind off yourself by helping a friend.[2]

Daily Coping Inventory

There are many ways to cope with stress. Below is a "Coping Inventory" that identifies various ways to deal with stress. One the right half there is a spot to check which coping method you used on a given day.[3] The point is to break the routine and spend time doing fun and relaxing things.

	S	M	T	W	T	F	S
Exercised							
Did abdominal breathing							
Did mental relaxation							
Meditated (try reading a few Bible verses each day)							
Prayed							
Did muscle relaxation							
Read a book							
Did painting or drawing							
Cooked for fun							
Took a warm bath, went swimming or to a spa							
Listened to quiet music							

2. "Stress Without Distress," 48.

3. This daily coping inventory was provided by the Bozeman, Montana, Cooperative Extension Service bulletin, "Stress Without Distress," 57.

Did something for others						
Gardened						
Talked it out						
Took a nap						
Played a musical instrument						
Received family support						
Met with social group						
Took a walk						
Practiced assertiveness						
Re-set priorities						
Revised daily schedule						
Spent some time alone						
Took a break from my routine						
Remembered, "What difference will it make seventy-five years from now?"						
Spent time doing something I enjoy—just for me						
Bought something new						
Went out to dinner						
Other:						
Other:						

Plan of Action

It's important to follow through with a specific plan of action. You may put together your own plan or use the four steps here.

1. Complete the stress diary each day for two weeks.

2. Practice personally selected coping strategies daily.

3. Include twenty to thirty minutes of moderate exercise daily.

4. Attempt to identify when you're feeling anxiety and utilize a coping strategy at that time.

My Reward:

If I successfully complete the record-keeping component of this two-week program, and work towards altering the effects of anxiety and stress in my life, my reward will be:

_____

_____

_____

_____

_____

_____

_____

_____

This reward will be received on:_____
Signature: _____
Signature of spouse or partner:_____

Personal Coping Inventory

Simply follow the instructions for each of the 14 items listed below. When you have completed all of the items, total your points and place that score in the box provided:

	Personal Coping Inventory
	Give yourself 10 points if you feel that you have a supportive family around you.
	Give yourself 10 points if you actively pursue a hobby.
	Give yourself 10 points if you belong to some social or activity group that meets at least once a month (other than your family).
	Give yourself 15 points if you are within five pounds of your ideal bodyweight, considering your height and bone structure.
	Give yourself 15 points if you practice some form of real relaxation at least three times a week.

	Give yourself 5 points for each time you exercise 20 to 30 minutes or longer during the course of an average week.
	Give yourself 5 points for each nutritionally balanced and wholesome meal you consume during the course of an average day.
	Give yourself 5 points if you do something that you really enjoy that is "just for you" during the course of an average week.
	Give yourself 10 points if you have some place in your home that you can go in order to relax and/or be yourself.
	Give yourself 10 points if you practice time management techniques in your family life.
	Subtract 10 points for each pack of cigarettes you smoke during the course of an average day.
	Subtract 5 points for each evening during the course of an average week that you take any form of medication or chemical substance (including alcohol) to help you sleep.
	Subtract 10 points for each day during the course of an average week that you consume any form of medication or chemical substance (including alcohol) to reduce your anxiety or just calm you down.
	Subtract 5 points for each evening during the course of an average week that you bring home work that is meant to be done at your place of employment.
	Total:

Now calculate your total score. A perfect score would be 115 points. If you scored in the 50 to 60 range you probably have an adequate collection of coping strategies for most common sources of stress. However, you should keep in mind that the higher your score the greater your ability to cope with stress in an effective and healthful manner.[4]

4. The personal coping inventory and its scoring were provided by the Bozeman, Montana, Cooperative Extension Service bulletin, "Stress Without Distress," 40.

10

Avoid Materialism

Look at the birds of the air; they do not sow or reap or store away in barns, and yet your heavenly Father feeds them. Are you not much more valuable than they? Who of you by worrying can add a single hour to his life? And why do you worry about clothes? See how the lilies of the field grow. They do not labor or spin. Yet I tell you that not even Solomon in all his splendor was dressed like one of these. If that is how God clothes the grass of the field, which is here today and tomorrow is thrown into the fire, will he not much more clothe you, O you of little faith? So do not worry, saying, "What shall we eat?" or "What shall we drink?" or "What shall we wear?" For the pagans run after all these things, and your heavenly Father knows that you need them. But seek first his kingdom and his righteousness, and all these things will be given to you as well. Therefore do not worry about tomorrow, for tomorrow will worry about itself. Each day has enough trouble of its own. (Matt 6:26–34)

MISPLACED SECURITY

A s we age it is easy to lose focus and forget the biblical mandates that remind us to avoid the temptation of materialism. This last chapter presents a caution to those over age fifty to guard against a preoccupation with materialism.

Somehow, our society has gripped us with the lure of "things." If ever there was a time to learn the importance of steadiness, stability, staying the course, and not being swayed off course, it is in our second half of life. Many young people are lured to materialism. Amazingly, as reported by *USA Today*, "household debt for those sixty-five and older is skyrocketing—up 164 percent on average in eight years, to $20,302.[1]

The story is told of a man who worked at the Post Office, whose job it was to process all the mail that had addresses that could not be read. One day, a letter came to his desk addressed in shaky handwriting to God. He thought he should open it. He opened it and read:

> Dear God,
>
> I am a 93-year-old widow, living on a very small pension. Yesterday someone stole my purse. It has $100 in it, which was all the money I had until my next pension check. Next Sunday is Christmas, and I had invited two of my friends over for dinner. Without that money, I have nothing to buy food. I have no family to turn to, and you are my only hope. Can you please help me?
> Sincerely, Edna

The postal worker was touched. He showed the letter to his fellow workers. Each of them dug into their wallets and came up with a few dollars. By the time he made the rounds, he had collected $96, which they put into an envelope and sent to the woman.

The rest of the day, all of the workers felt a warm glow for the kind thing they had done. Christmas came and went.

1. Dugas, "American Seniors Rack Up Debt," http://www.usatoday.com/money/perfi/retirement/2002-04-25-elderly-debt.htm.

A few days later another letter to God came from the old lady. All of the workers gathered around while the letter was opened. It read:

> Dear God,
>
> How can I ever thank you enough for what you did for me? Because of your gift of love, I was able to fix a glorious dinner for my friends. We had a very nice day and I told my friends of your wonderful gift. By the way, there was $4 missing. I think it must have been those thieves at the Post Office!
> Sincerely, Edna

In his book, *The Joys of Successful Aging*, George Sweeting gives some insight from 1 John 2:16: "For all that is in the world, the lust of the flesh, and the lust of the eyes, and the pride of life, is not of the Father, but is of the world" (KJV). Sweeting writes, "I believe that the sin of youth is, 'the lust of the flesh,' often referred to as 'sex'. . . . During the middle years many wrestle with the 'pride of life'. . . . But what is the sin of old age? Greed. The accumulation of things. The quest for more. The push for security. Old age confuses *having* with *being*. However, what you *are* beats what you *have*, any day."[2]

In Acts 10 we read about a man named Cornelius. Cornelius was a blessing to others and ended up being greatly blessed himself. He was the first Gentile Christian. Up to this point in the story of the church, the gospel had been preached only to Jews, Jewish proselytes, and Samaritans. However, in Acts 10 we meet Cornelius, a Roman! Christians were either Jewish converts or at least half-Jews (like the Samaritan converts and the Ethiopian eunuch). Now Cornelius, a Gentile, a Roman, hears the gospel and accepts Christ.

2. Sweeting, *Joys of Successful Aging*, 106.

BE OPEN, AWARE, AND SENSITIVE

From this story we may learn three important lessons:

1. We should be open to God's leading—God is a God of miracles.

2. We should be aware of needs of those around us—We are blessed to be a blessing to others.

3. We should be sensitive to what matters to God—Remember the two key words, perspective and balance.

In the early church, Satan failed trying to silence the witness of the believers. However, Satan did not give up. Satan's first approach was often to attack the church from outside. Arrests and threats frightened the leaders. Then Satan attacked *from the inside*. Satan is clever indeed. Scripture tells us that Satan is a "roaring lion" (1 Pet 5:8). Satan is like a "deceiving serpent"; Satan is called an "angel of light" (2 Cor 11:3, 13–14). Never forget the power we have in Christ to fight temptation. There is a basic biblical principle throughout scripture that I call unified commitment. That principle says: "Oneness of heart and mind brings unity and strength."

As we put this in our twenty-first-century culture context, remember that oneness of heart and mind brings greatness of power and witness. Think of family, neighbors, and friends as your partners in accountability and use that accountability, with the help of God, to turn away from temptations that present themselves. Our gifts to the Lord's work and to other people are building treasures in heaven.

In Luke 14:11 we read: "For all those who exalt themselves will be humbled, and those who humble themselves will be exalted." Phillips translation of the Bible puts it this way: "For everyone who makes himself important will become insignificant, while the man who makes himself insignificant will find himself important."

The lure of man's praises and materialism sit so strongly at the core of today's culture that sometimes we accept it as truth, when in fact it is a snare. It becomes important that we use our investment strategies wisely to help avoid the temptation of materialism.

We have God's resources available to us! There are tangible resources like our material and financial resources, and there are intangible resources like our talents, abilities, and spiritual ministry gifts. All of our resources are the result of God's favor and blessing, not personal achievement. In Luke 12:48 our Lord made an interesting statement about stewardship of resources: "From everyone who has been given much, much will be demanded; and from the one who has been entrusted with much, much more will be asked." Within this passage there are at least three biblical strategies:

1. Cheerful giving accomplishes eternal things.

2. Spending reasonably helps us keep *perspective* and *balance* toward meeting our personal needs.

3. Saving methodically provides a plan for meeting future needs.[3]

Especially in the mature years of life we should enjoy things, but not cherish them, and we should give joyfully, not reluctantly. Jesus said:

Matthew 6:19–21: "Do not store up for yourselves treasures on earth, where moth and rust destroy, and where thieves break in and steal. But store up for yourselves treasures in Heaven, where moth and rust do not destroy, and where thieves do not break in and steal. For where your treasure is, there your heart will be also.

3. Nowery, *33 Laws of Stewardship,* and Sutherland, *Stewardship of Life.*

1 John 2:15: "Do not love the world or anything in the world. If anyone loves the world, the love of the Father is not in him."

Luke 9:25: "What good is it for someone to gain the whole world, and yet lose or forfeit his very self?"

We serve an amazing, awesome God. He can take anything and use it for his glory. He is the multiplier; the God of miracles.

In the early part of the twentieth century, John D. Rockefeller was the richest man in the world. His businesses accounted for one of every thirty dollars generated in the entire United States economy.[4] In today's currency that would be equal to a fortune ten times greater than Bill Gates. Rockefeller died in 1937. A newspaper artist drew a cartoon that posed the question: "How much did he leave?" The answer in the next panel said simply: "He left it all."[5] So it is with each of us—we leave it all. In Luke 16 Jesus gives a parable with four lessons about life.

Jesus was always asking questions—probing questions for sure. Jesus's greatest teachings were characterized with his asking penetrating questions. Luke 16, a familiar story, is about a steward who is accused by his master of wasting the goods entrusted to him. As Jesus talked the disciples listened. They realized that he was applying it to them.

The first lesson in this parable is that if a person has been loaned something, someone else is the owner.

In Luke 16:1 the story about a foolish steward begins. A steward is someone who manages another's wealth. He doesn't own the wealth—just manages it. The most important quality is faithfulness. When he or she looks at the riches, it must be remembered that they belong to owner. The person

4. Ibid., 11.
5. Ibid.

mentioned in this story forgets this. This person begins to act as if it were his. However, before we judge him too quickly, how about us?

The second lesson in this parable is that since God is the owner of all things, we are the trustees of what we are, what we have, and what we can become.

How aware am I that God is the owner of all things? I am only the trustee of what I am, what I have, and what I can become.

The third lesson in this parable is that we must give an account of our privileges and opportunities. In Luke 16:10–13 we read: "Whoever can be trusted with very little can also be trusted with much, and whoever is dishonest with very little will also be dishonest with much. So if you have not been trustworthy in handling worldly wealth, who will trust you with true riches? If you have not been trustworthy with someone else's property, who will give you property of your own? No servant can serve two masters. Either he will hate the one and love the other, or he will be devoted to the one and despise the other. You cannot serve both God and Money."

We are managers of a trust. Each day is an opportunity for service and stewardship. Money is a means to an end, not an end in itself. Wise stewards are guided by lordship, not *hoard-ship*. Lordship means seeking God in all areas of life including, and perhaps especially, our resources. Using our ministry gifts and financial resources for God's glory provide eternal gain by helping and encouraging others and we grow in the process. We grow into spiritual leaders. Richness toward God manifests itself by seeing everything as a gift from his hand. Richness toward God comes through seeking his direction before settling on a decision. Richness toward God comes through caring more about giving than getting. The economics of stewardship is governed by the mathematics of the supernatural.

The apostle Paul wrote in 1 Corinthians 4:2 (KJV): "Moreover it is required in stewards that one be found faithful." In his book *The Joys of Successful Aging,* George Sweeting has a chapter titled, "Do Your Giving While You're Living." I like that idea. Sweeting says, "Giving is an essential part of being alive. Dead things may accumulate but they can't grow. Only living things . . . grow."[6] What an interesting thought and how true that is. Sweeting goes on to write, "William Gladstone, the brilliant British statesman, said concerning giving, 'There is no merit in a man leaving money in his will; he has simply got to leave it. The time to administer your trust . . . is while you are still living.'"[7]

As you think about the temptation of materialism, be aware of the subtle influence of the rugged individualism experienced today. Especially in our Western culture we believe that we can do it on our own and have a sort of "get what you can" mentality. I remember a friend of mine having a bumper sticker that read, "The one with the most toys at the end wins." Society pulls us toward materialism.

Temptation of Materialism

Questions to think about as you consider the temptation of materialism:

1. In what specific ways has the rugged individualism of our culture affected the way you regard your wealth and possessions?

2. How has rugged individualism affected your participation in the church?

6. Sweeting, *Joys of Successful Aging,* 105.
7. Ibid.

3. Why is effective spiritual leadership important for every church?

4. How do 1 Corinthians 4:2 and Luke 16:10–13 portray effective spiritual leadership?

Life seems to be filled with accumulating too much "stuff." When adults transition from full-time work they sometimes think of having less, not more. They may want to downsize for a simpler life. Priorities begin to change, especially when the time comes to face the reality of getting physically weaker. Ultimately, people need to accept the fact that they need help.

You have probably read the little humorous clipping titled "stuff"[8]:

Once each year I start stirring in all my stuff. There is closet stuff, drawer stuff, attic stuff, and basement stuff. I separate the good stuff from the bad stuff. Then I stuff the bad stuff anywhere the stuff is not too crowded until I decide if I will need the bad stuff.

When the Lord calls me home, my children will want the good stuff, but the bad stuff, stuffed wherever there is room among all the other stuff, will be stuffed in bags and taken to the dump where all the other people's stuff has been taken.

Whenever we have company, they always bring bags and bags of stuff. When I visit my son, he always moves his stuff so I will have room for my stuff. My daughter-in-law always clears a drawer of her stuff so I will have room for my stuff. Their stuff and my stuff . . . it would be so much easier to use their stuff and leave my stuff at home with the rest of my stuff. Last year I had an extra closet built so I could have

8. Based on the late comedian George Carlin's stand-up routine, "stuff," the text of which appears online: http://www.writers-free-reference.com/funny/story085.htm.

a place for all the stuff too good to throw away and too bad to keep with the good stuff. You may not have this problem, but I seem to spend a lot of time with stuff . . . food stuff, cleaning stuff, medicine stuff, clothes stuff, and outside stuff. Whatever would life be like if we didn't have all this stuff?

Now there is all that stuff we use to make us smell better than we do naturally. There is stuff to make us look younger. Stuff to make us healthier. Stuff to hold us in, stuff to fill us out. There is stuff to read, stuff to play with, stuff to entertain us and stuff to eat. We stuff ourselves with the food stuff.

Our lives are filled with stuff . . . good stuff, bad stuff . . . little stuff . . . big stuff . . . useful stuff . . . junky stuff . . . and everyone's stuff. When we leave all our stuff and go to Heaven, whatever happens to our stuff won't matter. We will then have the good stuff God has prepared for us in Heaven—perfect stuff.

Steps to Avoid Materialism

Taking the steps below will assist you in assuring that you do not fall into the temptation of preoccupation with materialism.

- Become better informed about God's wonderful promises. Reflect on his goodness.

- Praise the Lord and give thanks. Be thankful for the simplest things in life.

- Set some new goals for myself with God's direction.

- Find a biblical support group with Christian friends to help me grow.

- Claim the Holy Spirit's power in my life.

- Thank God for the glory that is ahead for me in heaven.

Downsizing and Relocation Strategies

Many people have accumulated too many things and when the time comes to downsize, they are have a huge challenge. Before concluding this chapter and this book, I would like to share a few relocation strategies. Selling your home can be a positive and rewarding experience, if you have the right information and resources to properly manage the process. The difference between success and failure can often be measured by the level of planning and amount of attention given to the details. Most states have an agency on aging that will provide helpful information. One such agency is the Area Agency on Aging (www.aaaphx.org). One of the many helpful articles in their book *AZSeniors Guide to Housing & Care*, is Connie Swenson's article, "Moving and Downsizing." It offers a wonderful checklist to help you in the relocation process.[9]

To insure that your experience is as smooth and stress-free as possible, you need proven strategies that can recognize and accommodate even the smallest details. Selling your home is a process—not a transaction. The process should begin with an evaluation of your needs, desires, and abilities and include those of your spouse, family, and friends. Developing clear goals and realistic expectations improves your likelihood for success. To help you initiate this process there are some questions to consider.

Why am I selling my home?

- Lifestyle change such as desire for Independent Community Living

- Require some sort of assistance such as Assisted Living or Skilled Nursing Care

- Looking for more amenities, services, or social

9. Swenson, "Moving and Downsizing," 44.

atmosphere

- Friends or neighbors have moved away
- Current home is too large for your needs
- Need money/equity from home
- Unable to take care of home
- Tired of the maintenance associated with home ownership
- Want to live in a place that you can "lock and leave"[10]

Is my home ready to sell?

- Fix items that require repair. They may appear more significant to prospective buyers.

- Remove furniture or personal items that are not necessary. A large home appears smaller with too much furniture, so you may want to consider temporary storage.

- Apply a fresh coat of paint to your walls if necessary. This is often the least expensive and most beneficial improvement you can make.

- Collect your warranty and operation manuals for your home and major appliances that will remain with the home. Perspective buyers may find this information very valuable.

- First and last impressions are critical. Don't ignore the exterior of your home.

- Locate important documents regarding your home such as title, loan information, tax records, and past utility bills.

- Ask a friend or realtor to walk through your home

10. Ibid.

using their eyes, ears, nose, and touch. An honest opinion may save you a lot of time and money.[11]

What are some of the ancillary issues that need to be considered?

- Establish a new forwarding address with the postal service.
- Complete a change of address form with your bank, previous employers, credit card companies, pension, Social Security Administration, etc.
- Redirect magazine, newspaper, and other subscription items to your new address.
- Change driver's license and discuss potential adjustments that may need to be made to your auto insurance.
- Sell or donate your vehicle if it is no longer needed.[12]

Fishing Village

One of my favorite little clippings is "Fishing Village":

An American investment banker was at the pier of a small coastal Mexican village when a small boat with just one fisherman docked. Inside the small boat were several large yellow fin tuna. The American banker complimented the Mexican fisherman on the quality of his fish and asked how long it took to catch them.

The Mexican replied, "Only a little while." The American then asked why didn't he stay out longer and catch more fish? The Mexican said he had enough to support his family's immediate needs. The American then asked, "But what do you do with the rest of your time?"

11. Ibid.
12. Ibid.

The Mexican fisherman said, "I sleep late, fish a little, play with my children, take a siesta with my wife Maria, stroll into the village each evening where I sip wine and play guitar with my amigos. I have a full and busy life."

The American scoffed, "I am a Harvard MBA and I could help you. You should spend more time fishing and with the proceeds, buy a bigger boat. With the proceeds from the bigger boat, you could buy several boats; eventually you would have a fleet of fishing boats. Instead of selling your catch to a middleman, you would sell directly to the processor, eventually opening your own cannery. You would control the product, processing, and distribution. You would need to leave this small coastal fishing village and move to Mexico City, then LA, and eventually New York City where you will run your expanding enterprise."

The Mexican fisherman asked, "But, how long will this all take?" To which the American replied, "15–20 years." "But what then?" The American laughed and said that's the best part. "When the time is right, you would announce an IPO and sell your company stock to the public and become very rich. You would make millions." "Millions . . . Then what?" The American said, "Then you would retire. Move to a small coastal fishing village where you would sleep late, fish a little, play with your kids, take a siesta with your wife, stroll to the village in the evenings where you could sip wine and play your guitar with your amigos."[13]

TEN HELPFUL AND PRACTICAL STEPS TO *AGING SUCCESSFULLY*

As we come to the end of this book I hope the ten steps shared will prove helpful and practical as you age.

13. Author unknown. As told online: http://www.noogenesis.com/pineapple/fisherman.html.

1. Keep perspective

2. Stay balanced

3. Enjoy midlife

4. Prepare for the later years

5. Focus on the biblical view

6. Understand loss and grief

7. Claim God's promises

8. Keep your spirits high

9. Relieve anxiety

10. Avoid materialism

In the Old Testament, pronouncing God's favor on the people was important. The priest was to use a formula for blessing the people. The blessing given communicated the desire of the Lord to invest his people with his name. He alone can bless his people, keep them, look on them with favor (make his face shine and turn his face toward them), be gracious to them, and give them peace. As you continue to age, may you truly age successfully and find peace in God. May you experience his full blessing upon your life.

> "The LORD bless you and keep you; the LORD make his face shine upon you and be gracious to you; the LORD turn his face toward you and give you peace." So they will put my name on the Israelites, and I will bless them. (Num 6:24–27)

Appendix A

Anxiety

Anxiety Disorders Association of America: http://www.adaa. org/. Provides resources on various forms of anxiety conditions. Includes comments on a message board and research information for professionals.

Depression

About Depression: http://www.depression.about.com/ Provides practical details about living with depression. Includes advice on depression disorders and treatment, on suicide, and on seeking help.

National Foundation for Depressive Illness: www.depression.org. Aims to educate the public about depressive illness. Presents a list of common symptoms and tips to help combat depression.

Caregiving

Children of Aging Parents: http://www.careguide.net/careguide.cgi/caps/capshome.htm. Provides referrals for attorneys, retirement communities, medical insurance, and respite care. Presents opportunities to learn about educational outreach efforts.

American College of Physicians Home Care Guide: http://www.acponline.org/patients_families/end_of_life_issues/cancer/. ACP offers an outline for persons with cancer and life-limiting conditions. Gives practical advice for caretakers as well as those who are facing death.

Alzheimer's

Alzheimer's Association: http://www.alz.org. Chicago-based volunteer group provides caregiver resources, chapter locations, and treatment and research information.

919 North Michigan Ave.
Suite 1000
Chicago, IL 60611
800–272–3900

Christian Online Information

Christianity.com: http://forums.christianity.com/. Provides substantial information and online chat room.

Stephen Ministries: http://www.stephenministries.org/. Provides distinctively Christian caregiving for people going through difficult times or who are otherwise in need of support in their lives.

Hospice

American Hospice Foundation: http://www.americanhospice.org. Organization is dedicated to caring for those where cure is no longer possible. Find publications, training workshops, and a hospice directory.

Hospice Association of America: http://www.nahc.org/haa/. Offers guidelines and resources for the hospice industry, including consumer information, education opportunities, and news.

Domestic Violence

American Bar Association: www.abanet.org/domviol/home. html. Presents the Commission on Domestic Violence Directory from the American Bar Association Commission on Domestic Violence. Includes links to shelters and support groups.

National Domestic Violence Hotline: http://www.thehotline. org/. Lists the national toll-free telephone number that offers support to domestic violence victims and their families. Offers shelter referrals and safety tips.

Funeral Planning

Federal Trade Commission. Funerals: A Consumer Guide: http://www.ftc.gov/bcp/edu/pubs/consumer/products/ pro19.shtm. Contains advice for consumers on funeral costs and industry regulations.

FuneralPlan.com. Funeral Planning Step by Step: http:// www.funeralplan.com/funeralplan/about/howto.html. Offers advice on all aspects of funeral planning from making a will to choosing a type of ceremony.

Bereavement

Bereaved Parents of the USA: http://www.bereavedparent-susa.org. Nationwide network organizes meetings for parents, grandparents, and siblings of a deceased child. Offers a section for the newly bereaved.

Death and Dying Grief Support: http://www.death-dying. com. Submit a question to a grief expert, read over past newsletters, discuss terminal illness and legal issues. Offers a section for teens.

Grief and Loss Support. American Association of Retired Persons: http://www.griefandloss.org. AARP offers resources to help individuals and families grieve the loss of a loved one, such as a child, spouse, sibling, or parent. Offers articles and advice.

Divorce

Action for Children: http://www.actionforchildren.org.uk/ our-services/family-support/targeted-intervention/mediation. Provides resources to children, teens, and parents for dealing with divorce. Offers the opportunity to participate in a survey.

Fresh Start Seminars: http://hstrial-frobinson2.homestead. com/. Christian group provides seminars and support groups for adults and children dealing with divorce. Presents a discussion forum and an event schedule.

Death of a Child

Janet Tischler, prenatal bereavement consultant
Miscarriage Infant Death Stillbirth
16 Cresent Dr.
Parsippany, NM 07054
201–966–6437

The Compassionate Friends National Headquarters
PO Box 3696
Oak Brook, IL 60522
312–990–0010

Kubler–Ross Center
South Route 616
Headwaters, VA 24442
703-396-3441

St. Francis Center
5417 Sherier Place, NW
Washington, DC 20016
202-363-8500

Make Today Count
168 Panoramic
Camdenton, MO 65065
314-346-6644

The Dougy Center for Grieving Children
3909 SE 52nd Ave.
PO Box 86852
Portland, OR 97286
503-775-5683

Books to help grandparents with Children ages 3–7

Buscaglia, Leo. *Freddie the Leaf.* New York: Holt, Rinehart, and Winston, 1982.
Harris, Audrey. *Why Did He Die?* Minneapolis, MN: Lerner Publications, 1965.
Viorst, Judith. *The Tenth Good Thing about Barney.* New York: Atheneum, 1972.
Stein, Sarah B. *About Dying.* New York: Walker and Company, 1974.

Books to help grandparents with children ages 8–14

Fassler, Joan. *My Grandpa Died Today.* New York: Behavioral Publications, 1971.

LeShan, Eda. *Learning to say Good-By*. New York: Macmillan Publishing, 1972.

Corley, Elizabeth. *Tell Me About Death; Tell Me About Funerals*. Santa Clara, CA: Grammatical Sciences, 1973.

L'Engle, Madeleine. *A Ring of Endless Light*. New York: Farrar, Straus, Giroux, 1980.

Suicide

American Foundation for Suicide Prevention: http://www. afsp.org.

WEB SITES AND RESOURCES

Access America for Seniors: http://www.seniors.gov. Provides government services electronically by linking to federal government information that pertains to the concerns of senior adults.

Administration on Aging: http://www.aoa.dhhs.gov. Serves as a gateway site for the large amount of senior-related information on the Internet.

American Association of Retired Persons (AARP): http://www.aarp.org. Provides in-depth information on a variety of senior-related concerns.

Medical Rights Center: http://www.medicarerights.org/. Provides free counseling services to Medicare beneficiaries who cannot afford private assistance.

National Senior Citizens Law Center: http://nsclc.org. Focuses on legal issues that affect the security and welfare of older persons with limited income.

Getting Started in Senior Adult Ministry

SeniorLaw: http://www.seniorlaw.com. Includes information about elder law, Medicare, Medicaid, estate planning, trusts, and the rights of the elderly and disabled.

Social Security Online: http://www.ssa.gov. The official web site of the Social Security Administration.

Third Age: http://www.thirdage.com. An online magazine to help seniors enjoy the best years of their lives.

Christian Association Serving Adult Ministries (CASA): http://www.gocasa.org. Presents information for the purpose of equipping and encouraging leaders aged fifty and beyond.

Total Living Network: http://www.sl50.org. The parent company of CASA, this organization provides tools for individuals in the second half of life.

Building Church Leaders: http://www.buildingchurchleaders.com/articles/2010/olderadultministryeffective.html. This site is a partnership between Significant Living and Christianity Today International with many helpful articles.

Halftime: http://www.halftime.org. Provides information about making adjustments to find more significance in the second half of life.

Twenty Suggested Sites for Making Retirement more Meaningful

Finishers Project works with many mission organizations: http://finishers.org/

Business at Missions (BAM): www.crossworld.org

Global Media Outreach (GMO): www.GMOJoinUs.com

Gospel for Asia: www.winasia.org

Grace International Ministries: http://www.grace-international-ministries.org/

Habitat for Humanity (HFHI): www.habitat.org

International Ministries: http://www.internationalministries.org/

Campus Crusade for Christ International: http://www.ccci.org/

Jews for Jesus: www.jewsforjesus.org

Leadership Development International (LDI): www.ldichina.com

Living Water Quilts: www.LivingWaterQuilts.org

Mission Aviation Fellowship (MAF): www.maf.org

Operation Mobilisation (OM): www.om.org

Partners International: www.partnersintl.org

Reach Across: www.reachacross.net

Serving in Mission (SIM): www.sim.org

Teach Overseas: www.TeachOverseas.org

World Concern: www.worldconcern.org

World Vision: www.Worldvision.org

Wycliffe Bible Translators: www.wycliffe.org

RECOMMENDED BOOKS

Bourke, Dale Hanson. *Second Calling: Finding Passion and Purpose for the Rest of Your Life*. Mayfield Heights, OH: Integrity Books, 2006.

Buechner, Frederick. *The Sacred Journe*. New York: Harper, 1982.

Buford, Bob. *Finishing Well*. Wake Forest, NC: Integrity Publishers, 2004.

Buford, Bob. *Halftime*. Grand Rapids, MI: Harper and Collins, 1994.

Carlson, Eric M., and Hsiao, Katharine, Bau. *Baby Boomer's Guide to Nursing Home Care*. New York: Taylor Trade Publishing, 2006.

Carter, Jimmy. *The Virtues of Aging*. New York: Ballantine, 1998.

Dychtwald, Ken. *Age Wave*. New York: Bantam Books, 1990.

Fischer, Kathleen. *Winter Grace*. Nashville: Upper Room Books, 1998.

Freedman, Marc. *Prime Time: How Baby Boomers Will Revolutionize Retirement and Transform America*. Civic Ventures. San Francisco: PublicAffairs, 1999.

Gallagher, David P. "20 Tips for Seniors Groups." In *Small Group Ministry in the 21st Century*, ed. Brad Lewis, 220–25. Loveland, CO: Group Publishing, 2005.

Gallagher, David P. "Five Ideas for Caring for Seniors." In *Outreach Ministry in the 21st Century: The Encyclopedia of Practical Ideas*, ed. Carl Simmons, 204–5. Loveland, CO: Group Publishing, 2006.

Gallagher, David P. *Healing Takes Time*. Collegeville, MN: Liturgical Press, 2005.

Gallagher, David P. "Ideas for Later-in-Life Marriage: Coping with Health Issues and Keeping Long Term Marriages Alive." In *Marriage Ministry in the 21st Century*, ed. Brad Lewis, 173–76. Loveland, CO: Group Publishing, 2007.

Gallagher, David P. "Ideas to Get Small Groups Outreach-minded." In *Outreach Ministry in the 21st Century: The Encyclopedia of Practical Ideas*, ed. Carl Simmons, 194–95. Loveland, CO: Group Publishing, 2006.

Gallagher, David P. "Reminders for Dealing with Death and Funerals." In *Pastoral Ministry in the 21st Century: The Encyclopedia of Practical Ideas*, ed. Brad Lewis and Carl Simmons, 157–58.

Gallagher, David P. *Senior Adult Ministry in the 21st Century*. Eugene, OR: Wipf and Stock, 2006 (originally published by Group Publishing, 2002).

Gallagher David P. "Service Ideas for Older Adults." In *Outreach Ministry in the 21st Century: The Encyclopedia of Practical Ideas*, ed. Carl Simmons, 196–97. Loveland, CO: Group Publishing, 2006.

Gallagher, David P. "Tips for Hospital Visits." In *Pastoral Ministry in the 21st Century: The Encyclopedia of Practical Ideas*, ed. Brad Lewis and Carl Simmons, 155–56. Loveland, CO: Group Publishing, 2007.

APPENDIX A

Gambone, James. *ReFirement: A Boomer's Guide to Life After 50.* Minneapolis, MN: Kirk House Publishers, 2000.

Gillon, Steve. *Boomer Nation.* New York: Simon & Schuster, 2004.

Gilmore, John. *Ambushed at Sunset: Coping with Mature Adult Temptations.* San Antonio, TX: LangMarc Publishing, 1998.

Graham, Billy. *Nearing Home.* Nashville: Thomas Nelson, 2011.

Green, Brent. *Marketing to Leading-Edge Baby Boomers.* Ithaca, NY: Paramount Market Publishing, 2006.

Hanson, Amy. *Baby Boomers and Beyond.* San Francisco: Jossey-Bass, 2010.

Haugk, Kenneth C. *Christian Caregiving a Way of Life.* Minneapolis, MN: Augsburg Publishing, 1984.

Haugk, Kenneth C. *When and How to use Mental Health Resources.* St. Louis, MO: Stephen Ministries, 2000.

Hicks, Rick and Kathy. *Boomers, Xers, and Other Strangers.* Tyndale, 1999.

Hollis, James. *Finding Meaning in the Second Half of Life.* New York: Gotham Books, 2005.

Houston, James M., and Michael Parker. *A Vision for the Aging Church.* Downers Grove, IL: InterVarsity Press, 2011.

Kirkwood, Neville. *Pastoral Care in Hospitals.* Harrisburg, PA: Morehouse Publishing, 1995.

Knapp, James L. *The Graying of the Flock.* Orange, CA: Leafwood Publishers, 2003.

Knapp, James L. *Understanding the Generations.* San Diego, CA: Aventine Press, 2005.

Koenig, Harold G., and Andrew J. Weaver. *Pastoral Care of Older Adults.* Minneapolis, MN: Fortress Press, 1998.

Koenig, Harold G. *Purpose and Power in Retirement.* New York: Templeton Foundation Press, 2003.

Lustbader, Wendy. *Counting on Kindness: The Dilemmas of Dependency.* New York: The Free Press, 1991.

McIntosh, Gary L. *One Church Four Generations.* Grand Rapids, MI: Baker Books, 2002.

Moberg, David O. *Aging and Spirituality.* New York: Haworth Pastoral Press, 2001.

Morgan, Richard, ed. *Dimensions of Older Adult Ministry: A Handbook.* Louisville, KY: Witherspoon Press, 2006.

Oakes, Charles G. *Working the Gray Zone.* Franklin, TN: Providence House Publishers, 2000.

Peterson, Peter. *Gray Dawn.* New York: Random House, 1999.

Pipher, Mary. *Another Country: Navigating the Emotional Terrain of Our Elders.* New York: Riverhead Books, 1999.

Roof, Wade Clark. *Spiritual Marketplace: Baby Boomers and the Remaking of American Religion.* Princeton, NJ: Princeton University Press, 1999.

Rose, Jerry, and Shirley Rose. *GPS God's Plan for Significance.* Chicago: SigLivPublishing/Total Living Network, 2006.

Roszak, Theodore. *Longevity Revolution.* Albany, CA: Berkeley Hills Books, 2001.

Shaw, Eva. *What to do When a Loved One Dies.* Irvine, CA: Dickens Press, 1994.

Simmons, Henry, and Jane Wilson. *Soulful Aging: Ministry through the Stages of Adulthood.* Macon, GA: Smyth and Helwys Publishing, 2001.

Simpson, Carol. *At the Heart of Alzheimer's.* Toledo, OH: Manor Healthcare Corporation, 1996.

Smith, J. Walker, and Ann Clurman. *Generation Ageless.* New York: Harper Collins Books, 2007.

Solie, David. *How to Say It to Senior.* Upper Saddle River, NJ: Prentice Hall Press, 2004.

Sullender, R. Scott. *Losses in Later Life.* New York: Haworth Pastoral Press, 1999.

Sweeting, George. *The Joys of Successful Aging.* Chicago: Northfield Publishing, 2002

Vaillant, George E. *Aging Well.* Little, New York: Brown and Company, 2003.

Wiersbe, Warren, and David Wiersbe. *Ministering to the Mourning.* Chicago: Moody, 2006.

Young, David. *Celebrating the Rest of Your Life.* Minneapolis, MN: Augsburg Books, 2005.

Appendix B

Yearly Aging Journal

Use this yearly aging journal to put down your thoughts at the start of each year about how you feel about each of the categories: where you would like to live at the present time and in the future, whether you will want to or need to be involved in some sort of work, what activities you are or will be involved in, your financial thoughts and plans, etc.

Age	Living/ Housing	Family	Work	Activities	Financial	Spiritual
50–60						
60–70						
70–80						
80–90						
90+						

Family Information

	Name	Birth	SSN	Address	Phone
Husband					
Wife					
Child					
Sister					
Brother					
Parent					
In-Laws					
Other					
Other					
Other					

Names of Important People

Last Name	First Name	Address	City	State	Zip Code	Phone

APPENDIX B

Doctors, Clinics, and Hospitals

Doctor's Name	Type	Phone	Address	Remarks

Insurance

Type of Policy	Company	Number	Includes	Phone
Life Insurance				
Homeowner				
Automobile				
Health				
Other				

Professional Assistance

	Name	Telephone	Organization	Address
Church				
Investments				
Accountant				
Attorney				
Bank				
Mortgage				
Mortuary				
Other				

Location of Documents and Papers
(if other than this notebook)

	Type	Location
Budget	Monthly bills, payments, etc.	
Cards	Bank, clubs, stores, etc.	
Contracts	Addresses, phone listings, etc.	
Insurance	Life, car, home, etc.	
Investments	IRAs, stocks, bonds, etc.	
Medical	Doctors, hospitals, etc.	
Tax Papers	Filings, returns, etc.	
Other		

APPENDIX B

Assets

	Status
Primary Home	
Secondary Home	
Time-Share(s)	
Vehicle(s)	
Furniture	
Membership(s)	
Investment(s)	
Bank Account(s)	

Budget

Item	Cost
Home Mortgage	
Vehicle Mortgage or Lease	
Insurance (health)	
Insurance (long term care)	
Insurance (home)	
Electric	
Water	
Gas	
Telephone	
Cable TV	
Credit Union	
Bank (name and address)	
Credit Card (names)	
Department Store (card number)	
Church	
Doctor (name and specialty)	

Personal Planning Resources

Dentist	
Charity (name and address)	
Other	
Other	
Total:	$

Automatic Payments

Name of Institution	Address	Phone	E-Mail Address

APPENDIX B

Home Guidance

Description	Type of home, address, lot #, subdivision, area, according to book #, page #, records of _____ county, state of _____
Deed	Type of deed (joint tenancy, etc.), number, dated
Purchase	$_____ (estimate is fine)
Mortgage	Company, address, phone, number, balance as of date $_____
Improvements	List type and cost
House or Apartment Base Price	$ _____ (estimate is fine)

Funeral Arrangements

1. Pre-arrangements have been made with the following mortuary: _____

2. I/We DO NOT own a cemetery lot or columbarium space (select one)

3. We wish to be buried in the _____ Cemetery with Graveside committal service with/without Military honors OR _____
Memorial Service: _____
(A detailed outline for Memorial Services is found on the following pages.)

4. I/We wish to have a public memorial service at _____ and also at _____ with/without casket.

5. I/We wish to have _____ and _____ conduct the service.

6. I/We desire that the Military or TROA conduct the Military portion of the service (retired military only).

7. I/We request that the following close friends have an opportunity to speak (if they desire): _____

_____

8. I/We desire that the following hymns to be included: ___

_____

9. I/We wish the service(s) to be light and uplifting and not, if at all possible, gloomy or morose.

10. Other desires: _____

_____

11. I/We request that memorial gifts be given to: _____

_____

Sample Memorial Service

Prelude:_____

Greeting:_____

Scripture:_____

Solo:_____

First personal witness (if desired):_____

Second personal witness (if desired):_____

Obituary/Eulogy (if desired):_____

Hymn:_____

Poem:_____

Prayer:_____

Message:_____

Military presentation (if retired military and if desired):

_____

Benediction:_____

Postlude:_____

Record of Notification of Death

Death certificates are obtained from the mortuary and should accompany many of these letters. It is suggested that you originally ask for ten copies of the certificate. More may be obtained at a later time if needed; however, it may take longer to receive them.

Letter Sent (name of organization)	Date sent

Notification of Death

Date:_____

Inside address:_____

Address of sender:_____

RE: Death of_____

Account number _____

This letter is to inform you that _____

_____, SSN _____, died on _____.

A copy of the death certificate is enclosed. I am the

_____ of _____.

My e-mail address is _____.

Please contact me if you have any questions regarding this notification.
Sincerely,
Enclosure:
Death Certificate
CC: _____

Veteran's Benefit Guidance (if applicable)

As an honorably discharged veteran from the military, you are entitled to:

1. A burial allowance limited to ($300) for expenses for burial and funeral

2. An allowance of ($150) payable toward burial plot, if a national cemetery is not used

3. A burial flag

4. A bronze memorial or headstone

5. A presidential memorial certificate

You will need to contact the nearest VA office. VA Regional Office: 1–800–827–1000, Benefits and Claims. The VA may also be contacted at www.va.gov.

The VA normally requests the following:

1. Death Certificate

2. Marriage Certificate

3. Birth Certificate

4. Form 214: Discharge Papers

5. Receipted itemized funeral bill

A non-service connected death may entitle the spouse to pension payments. The VA will determine eligibility.

Many valuable benefits are available to the survivors of a veteran whose death was the result of a service-connected disability. Therefore, any illness, injury, or condition that could even remotely be considered a factor in establishing a service-connected disability at the time of death should be made a matter of official record.

Even if one has already retired from the service, one is well advised to maintain a record of doctors, and apply for benefits under the Survivor's Benefits Act.

Military Service

Record of Service

Date Entered:_____

Separation Date:_____

Net Active Service:_____

Foreign Service:_____

Date of Pay Grade:_____

Discharge Papers (this is the most important military document needed):_____

Decorations, Medals, Ribbons (list all):_____

Military Education:_____

Current Military Health Care (hospitals, clinics, doctors, etc.):

_____

_____

Veteran's Benefits:_____

Clubs and Organizations

Name of Organization	Address	Phone

Credit Cards

Card Name	Number

Important Papers

Health Power(s) of Attorney_____

Living Will(s)_____

Insurance Policies_____

Last Will(s) and Testament(s)_____

Revocable Living Trust(s)_____

General Power(s) of Attorney_____

Specific Power(s) of Attorney_____

Clubs and Credit Cards_____

APPENDIX B

Listing of Gifted Items and to Whom Given_____

Pictures of Gifted Items_____

Bibliography

Arn, Charles, and Win Arn. *The New Senior*. Monrovia, CA: Institute for American Church Growth, 2004.

Burke, Larry K. "Preventing Depression." *AZSeniors Guide to Housing and Care*. Annual edition (2003) 62–64.

Collins, Gary. *How to Be a People Helper*. Santa Ana, CA: Vision House Publishers, 1976.

Dugas, Christine. "American Seniors Rack Up Debt Like Never Before." *USA Today*, April 24, 2002. No Pages. Online: http://www.usatoday.com/money/perfi/retirement/2002-04-25-elderly-debt.htm.

Dychtwald, Ken, and Joe Flower. *Age Wave*. New York: Bantam Books, 1990.

Gallagher, David. *Healing Takes Time*. Collegeville, MN: Liturgical Press, 2005.

———. "Marriage Matters." *Rev! Magazine* 10 no. 3 (Jan/Feb 2007) 22–23.

———. *Senior Adult Ministry in the 21st Century*. Eugene, OR: Wipf and Stock Publishers, 2006.

The Golden Years: Riding the Crest. Serendipity Support Group. Littleton, CO: Serendipity House, 1990.

Green, Brent. *Marketing to Leading-Edge Baby Boomers*. Ithaca, NY: Paramount Market Publishing, 2006.

Gutowski, Carolyn. *Grandparents Are Forever*. Mahwah, NJ: Paulist Press, 1994.

Hanson, Amy. *Baby Boomers and Beyond*. San Francisco, CA: Jossey-Bass, 2010.

Houston, James M., and Michael Parker. *A Vision for the Aging Church*. Downers Grove, IL: InterVarsity Press, 2011.

How Do I Find It? A Guide to Long/Short Term Care Options in the Northwest Valley. Surprise, AZ: Northwest Valley Regional Community Council, 1998.

Jackson, Edgar N. *For the Living*. Des Moines, IA: Meredith Publishing, 1963.

Jakes, P. David. *The Decision is Yours*. Nashville, TN: LifeWay Press, 1995.

Kennedy, John W. "A Senior Moment." *Christianity Today* 55 no. 12 (Dec 2011) 46–49.

Bibliography

Lane, Ken. "Graying around the Globe." *Focus on the Family* (Nov 2007) 10–11.

MacDonald, Gordon. *Who Stole My Church? What to Do When the Church You Love Tries to Enter the Twenty-first Century.* Nashville, TN: Thomas Nelson, 2007.

Manning, Doug. *The Gift of Significance.* Hereford, TX: In-Sight Books, 1992.

McIntosh, Gary L. *One Church Four Generations.* Grand Rapids, MI: Baker Books, 2002.

National Center for Elder Abuse. March 3, 1010 e-news. No Pages. Online: http://www.ncea.aoa.gov/Main_Site/pdf/publication/NCEAWhatIs Abuse-2010.pdf.

Nowery, Kirk. *The 33 Laws of Stewardship.* Camarillo, CA: Spire Resources, Inc. 2003.

"The Older Population: 2010." Webinar presented Nov. 30, 2011 by the U.S. Census Bureau. Online: http://2010.census.gov/news/pdf/20111130_slides.pdf.

"Redefining Retirement." Del Webb Corporation. VHS videotape. Phoenix, AZ: Del Webb, 1994.

"Report of the Second World Assembly on Ageing, Madrid, 8–12 April 2002." United Nations publication: Sales no. E.02.4.4, chap. 1, resolution 1, annex 2. No pages. Online: http://www.c-fam.org/docLib/20080625_Madrid_Ageing_Conference.pdf.

Rose, Jerry, and Shirley Rose. *GPS God's Plan for Significance.* Chicago: SigLiv

Smith, J. Walker, and Ann Clurman *Generation Ageless: How Baby Boomers are Changing the Way We Live Today . . . And They're Just Getting Started.* New York: Harper Collins, 2007.

Stedman, Ray. *Folk Psalms of Faith.* Glendale, CA: Regal Books, 1973.

Storm, Kay Marshall. *The Second Half Adventure.* Moody Publishers. Chicago: Moody, 2009.

"Stress Without Distress." Cooperative Extension Service, bulletin 1249. Bozeman, MT: Montana State University, 1981.

"Surprised by Suffering." The Lutheran Church, Missouri Synod. No pages. Online: http://www.lcms.org/page.aspx?pid=868.

Sutherland, Dave. *The Stewardship of Life.* Camarillo, CA: Spire Resources, 2004.

Sweeting, George. *The Joys of Successful Aging.* Chicago, IL: Northfield Publishing, 2002.

Swenson, Connie. "Moving and Downsizing." *AZSeniors Guide to Housing & Care.* Annual edition (2003) 44–45.

Veninga, Robert L. *Your Renaissance Years: Making Retirement the Best Years of Your Life.* Boston, MA: Little, Brown, 1991.